BON APPÉTIT®

Tastes *of the* World

THE CONDÉ NAST PUBLICATIONS INC.

Tastes of the World

INTRODUCTION

Leaf your way through any issue of *Bon Appétit*, and more likely than not you'll get the feeling that you're touring the world. Food, after all, is one of the great bonds shared by all people, and in the magazine, month after month, we celebrate that common connection by bringing to our readers the tastes of many lands.

That's the inspiration behind this *Tastes of the World* cookbook. On the following pages, you'll find a deliberately eclectic collection of fabulous recipes from around the world, all of which have appeared in *Bon Appétit* over the past several years.

While compiling these recipes, we were tempted at first to organize them by country or region. But, thinking hard about how you were most likely to use the book, we decided instead to present the chapters course by course and to tag each individual recipe with its place of origin. This approach makes for some delightful juxtapositions. In the "Appetizers & Beverages" chapter, for example, you'll discover smooth Middle Eastern dips close by robust Indian vegetable fritters, lively Mexican *quesadillas* and elegant French-style artichokes. The section on pastas–where, as you might expect, Italy is well represented–also includes recipes from Mexico, France, Greece and China. And "Desserts" offers perhaps the most whirlwind of tours, flying from Morocco to the Caribbean, from Spain to China and from England back home to the United States.

The result, we think, is a book you can use in any number of ways. Dip into it for a single recipe to make tonight's dinner different. Flip through its pages and consult the index to compose a special menu featuring a single cuisine. Or add a dash of creativity and create a multicultural extravaganza.

Whatever path you take, let us add one more ingredient, a salutation spoken wherever people of good taste gather to enjoy lovingly prepared food: *Bon Appétit!*

On the cover: Vegetable Platter with Cannellini Hummus, Pasta with Shrimp and Basil Vinaigrette, and Bruschetta with Olive Paste, Peppers and Goat Cheese.

Photography by Michael Lamotte

BON APPÉTIT®

Tastes *of the* World

CONTENTS

Appetizers & Beverages

Start the party with an international array of tempting dishes, from Middle Eastern Red Pepper Hummus to Indian Vegetable Patties, French Artichokes with Goat Cheese to all-American Grilled Oysters and Clams with Lime Butter. Add a soothing cup of Moroccan Mint Tea, a festive glass of Victorian "Eggnog" from England or a Very Special Champagne Cocktail from France, and your meal is off to a delightful start.

Appetizers

RED PEPPER HUMMUS

Teamed with pita bread triangles and a variety of raw vegetables, this Middle Eastern dip makes a great snack or hors d'oeuvre for a dinner party. Tahini is available at natural foods stores and some supermarkets.

MAKES ABOUT 2 CUPS

2 large garlic cloves, chopped
1 15-ounce can garbanzo beans (chickpeas), drained
⅓ cup tahini (sesame seed paste)
⅓ cup fresh lemon juice
½ cup chopped drained roasted red peppers from jar
Salt and pepper

With processor running, drop garlic through feed tube and mince. Scrape down sides of work bowl. Add chickpeas, tahini and lemon juice; process until mixture is smooth. Add roasted peppers; process until peppers are finely chopped. Season with salt and pepper. Transfer hummus to small bowl. *(Can be made 1 day ahead. Cover and chill. Bring to room temperature before serving.)*

CHEESE QUESADILLAS WITH SALSA VERDE

Crispy corn tortillas filled with Monterey Jack cheese and paired with a tomatillo salsa are an easy starter.

MAKES 8

8 teaspoons (about) vegetable oil
16 6-inch corn tortillas
2 cups shredded Monterey Jack cheese (about 8 ounces)

Salsa Verde (see recipe)

Heat 1 teaspoon oil in medium non-stick skillet over medium-high heat. Add 1 tortilla. Sprinkle tortilla with ¼ cup cheese. Top with another tortilla and press with spatula to compact. Cook until cheese melts and tortillas are crisp and light golden, about 2 minutes per side. Transfer to work surface. Repeat with remaining tortillas and cheese, adding more oil by teaspoonfuls as necessary.

Cut quesadillas into quarters; place on platter. Serve with Salsa Verde.

SALSA VERDE

Also terrific with tortilla chips.

MAKES ABOUT 4 CUPS

2 pounds fresh tomatillos,* husked, chopped
2 small onions, chopped
1 cup water

1 cup chopped fresh cilantro
4 jalapeño chilies, seeded, minced
2 garlic cloves, minced
Salt

Combine tomatillos, onions and water in heavy large saucepan. Boil until tomatillos are tender, stirring occasionally, about 5 minutes. Transfer mixture to processor; process until chunky puree forms. Chill until cool, about 1 hour. (*Can be made 1 day ahead. Cover and keep chilled.*)

Stir cilantro, chilies and garlic into salsa. Season to taste with salt.

A green tomato-like vegetable with a paper-thin husk. Available at Latin American markets and some supermarkets.

FRANCE

ARTICHOKES WITH GOAT CHEESE

An innovative first course.

6 SERVINGS

8 tablespoons fresh lemon juice
6 medium artichokes, tops and
   stems trimmed

8 ounces soft fresh goat cheese
   (such as Montrachet)
3 tablespoons whipping cream
3 teaspoons minced fresh thyme or
   1 teaspoon dried
2 large garlic cloves, pressed
   Salt and pepper

3 tablespoons butter
3 tablespoons olive oil

Bring large pot of water to boil. Add 2 tablespoons lemon juice to water. Add artichokes and cook until tender, about 25 minutes. Drain well. Cool completely. Using small spoon and keeping artichokes intact, carefully remove tiny center leaves and chokes.

Mix goat cheese, cream, 2 teaspoons thyme and garlic in small bowl. Season to taste with salt and pepper. Spoon mixture into center of artichokes, dividing equally. Place each artichoke in center of square piece of foil large enough to cover artichoke completely. Gather foil up around artichoke, twisting top of foil to secure. (*Can be prepared 1 day ahead. Refrigerate.*)

Preheat oven to 400°F. Place artichokes on baking sheet and bake until heated through, about 15 minutes. Melt butter in heavy small skillet. Add olive oil and remaining 6 tablespoons lemon juice and bring to simmer.

Remove from heat and stir in remaining 1 teaspoon thyme. Season to taste with salt and pepper. Unwrap artichokes. Place each in center of plate. Drizzle butter mixture around each and serve.

MIDDLE EAST

WILD RICE-STUFFED GRAPE LEAVES

White rice, currants and pine nuts also go into the filling for this regional specialty.

MAKES ABOUT 30

6 tablespoons olive oil
1 onion, chopped
2/3 cup (about 4½ ounces) Uncle
   Ben's Long Grain and Wild Rice
½ teaspoon ground allspice
1½ cups water
¼ cup dried currants

¼ cup pine nuts
   Salt and pepper

1 8-ounce jar grape leaves,* drained
¼ cup water

¼ cup fresh lemon juice

Fresh lemon wedges
Chopped fresh parsley

Heat 2 tablespoons oil in heavy medium saucepan over medium heat. Add onion and sauté until tender, about 5 minutes. Add rice and allspice and stir 30 seconds. Add 1½ cups water and currants and bring to boil. Reduce heat to low, cover and simmer until water is absorbed and rice is tender, about 20 minutes. Remove from heat.

Heat 1 tablespoon oil in heavy small skillet over medium-low heat. Add pine nuts and sauté until golden brown, about 6 minutes. Mix nut mixture into rice. Season with salt and pepper.

Bring large pot of water to boil. Add grape leaves and stir to separate. Turn off heat; let stand 1 minute. Drain. Rinse with cold water to cool; drain well.

Cover bottom of heavy large skillet or Dutch oven with about 10 grape leaves, pressing about 1 inch up sides of skillet. Arrange 1 leaf, vein side up, on work surface. Place 1 rounded tablespoon rice filling near stem. Fold in sides, then roll up jellyroll fashion. Repeat with remaining filling and leaves. Arrange stuffed leaves, seam side down, close together in leaf-lined skillet. Drizzle 3 tablespoons oil over. Add ¼ cup water and fresh lemon juice. Bring to boil. Reduce heat to medium-low, cover and cook 50 minutes. Cool completely. *(Grape leaves can be made 1 day ahead. Cover and refrigerate.)*

Arrange stuffed grape leaves on platter. Garnish with lemon and parsley.

*Available at Greek, Middle Eastern and most Italian markets.

INDIA

VEGETABLE PATTIES

MAKES ABOUT 12

1¼ cups fresh corn kernels or frozen, thawed
1 medium carrot, grated
1 medium russet potato, peeled, grated
½ medium onion, finely chopped
½ cup shredded fresh spinach leaves
6 tablespoons all-purpose flour
¼ cup frozen peas, thawed
¼ cup finely chopped fresh cilantro
1 jalapeño chili, seeded, minced
2 teaspoons minced garlic
1 teaspoon minced fresh ginger
1 teaspoon ground cumin
Salt and pepper
1 large egg, beaten to blend

1 tablespoon (or more) vegetable oil
Plain yogurt
Purchased Major Grey chutney

Mix first 12 ingredients in large bowl to blend. Season to taste with salt and pepper. Stir in egg. Form 3 tablespoons of mixture into 3-inch-diameter patty. Place on large baking sheet. Repeat with remaining mixture. Refrigerate until firm, about 1 hour.

Heat 1 tablespoon oil in heavy large nonstick skillet over medium heat. Cook vegetable patties in batches until golden, adding more oil as necessary, about 4 minutes per side. Serve with yogurt and chutney.

(Cover Recipe)

BRUSCHETTA WITH OLIVE PASTE, PEPPERS AND GOAT CHEESE

To make this easy appetizer even easier, substitute store-bought roasted red bell peppers for the home-roasted ones.

4 SERVINGS

2 small red bell peppers

8 4x2x½-inch slices country-style bread

10 teaspoons olivada*

4 ounces soft fresh goat cheese (such as Montrachet), crumbled
Pepper
Chopped fresh parsley

Char red bell peppers over gas flame or in broiler until blackened on all sides. Seal roasted bell peppers in paper bag and let stand 10 minutes. Peel and seed bell peppers. Cut bell peppers into ½-inch-wide strips.

Prepare barbecue (medium heat) or preheat broiler. Grill bread until golden brown, watching closely so that bread does not burn, about 2 minutes per side. Spread 1 side of each bread slice with 1 generous teaspoon olivada. Top with bell peppers, then cheese. Season with pepper. Sprinkle with chopped fresh parsley.

An olive spread, sometimes called black olive paste or cream, available at Italian markets and specialty foods stores. If unavailable, use pureed pitted brine-cured black olives.

FISHY BUSINESS

Norwegian smoked salmon makes a nice hors d'oeuvre when served on rye bread with dill and lemon, and is also delicious draped over potato pancakes as a first course.

(Cover Recipe)

VEGETABLE PLATTER WITH CANNELLINI "HUMMUS"

Hummus, a dip/spread traditional in many Middle Eastern countries, is usually made with chickpeas (garbanzo beans), but we use white beans here for a change of pace. It is delicious with steamed potatoes and artichokes as well as blanched broccoli, cauliflower and green beans. Partner it with olives, pita bread and stuffed grape leaves.

6 SERVINGS

HUMMUS

2 15-ounce cans cannellini (white kidney beans), rinsed, drained

½ cup fresh lemon juice

½ cup tahini* (sesame seed paste)

3 garlic cloves, minced

1½ teaspoons chili powder

2 tablespoons minced fresh thyme
Salt and pepper
Fresh thyme leaves

VEGETABLES

1 pound baby red-skinned potatoes
2 large artichokes
3 lemon halves

1 pound broccoli, cut into florets
1 head cauliflower, cut into florets
¾ pound green beans, trimmed

2 bunches baby carrots, peeled
　Pita bread, cut into triangles

FOR HUMMUS: Combine first 5 ingredients in processor; puree. If necessary, mix in enough water to thin to consistency of thick mayonnaise. Mix in 2 tablespoons minced thyme. Season with salt and pepper. Transfer to bowl. Sprinkle with fresh thyme leaves. (Can be made 1 day ahead. Cover and chill.)

FOR VEGETABLES: Steam potatoes until just tender, about 25 minutes. Transfer to bowl. Cut off stems of artichokes and rub cut surface with cut side of lemon. Cut artichokes lengthwise into quarters and rub cut surfaces with lemon. Cut out choke and rub

with lemon. Bring large pot of salted water to boil. Add 1 remaining lemon half and artichokes. Cover and boil until a leaf pulls off easily, about 35 minutes. Drain and cool.

Cook broccoli and cauliflower in large saucepan of boiling salted water until just tender, about 5 minutes. Using slotted spoon, transfer to bowl of cold water. Add green beans to same boiling water and cook until just tender, about 4 minutes. Drain. Rinse with cold water to stop cooking. Drain. (Can be prepared 1 day ahead. Wrap vegetables tightly and refrigerate.)

Arrange all vegetables on large platter. Serve with hummus and pita bread.

Available at Middle Eastern and natural foods stores and some supermarkets.

GRILLED OYSTERS AND CLAMS WITH LIME BUTTER

6 SERVINGS

1 cup (2 sticks) butter
2 tablespoons fresh lime juice
2 tablespoons grated lime peel
　Salt and pepper

18 fresh oysters in shells, scrubbed
18 fresh clams in shells, scrubbed

Melt butter in heavy small saucepan over low heat. Whisk in lime juice and lime peel. Season with salt and pepper. (Can be prepared 1 day ahead. Cover and refrigerate. Before using, melt over low heat, whisking constantly.)

Preheat barbecue (medium-high heat). Place shellfish on barbecue and grill until shells open, turning occasionally, about 5 minutes (discard any that do not open). Transfer oysters and clams to platter. Drizzle with lime butter.

MUSSELS WITH SHALLOTS AND THYME

6 SERVINGS

3 tablespoons extra-virgin olive oil
6 shallots, finely chopped
8 fresh thyme sprigs
2 bay leaves
1 cup dry white wine
1 cup bottled clam juice
¼ cup whipping cream
2 pounds mussels, scrubbed, debearded
Salt and pepper

Heat oil in large skillet over medium heat. Add shallots; sauté until softened, about 10 minutes. Add thyme, bay leaves, wine, clam juice and cream; bring to boil. Reduce heat; simmer until mixture is reduced to 1 cup, about 10 minutes. Add mussels, cover and simmer until mussels open, about 7 minutes; discard any mussels that do not open. Using tongs, divide mussels among bowls. Season broth with salt and pepper. Ladle broth over mussels.

YOGURT "CHEESE" WITH PITA AND OLIVES

This tangy, fresh yogurt "cheese"—known as labaneh—*vies for attention with hummus and tahini on the standard Israeli platter of* mezze, *or appetizers. Here it's seasoned with sesame seeds and spices, and drizzled with olive oil. Plan to start this the day before serving.*

MAKES ABOUT 2 CUPS

Cheesecloth

4 cups plain yogurt
(do not use low-fat or nonfat)

1 teaspoon sesame seeds
½ teaspoon salt
¼ teaspoon dried summer savory
⅛ teaspoon cayenne pepper
⅛ teaspoon ground cumin
2 tablespoons extra-virgin olive oil
Toasted pita bread triangles
Assorted olives

Set strainer over large bowl. Line strainer with 4 layers of cheesecloth, allowing 4 inches to extend over sides of strainer (do not let strainer touch bottom of bowl). Spoon yogurt into strainer. Gather cheesecloth together; fold over yogurt. Refrigerate at least 8 hours or overnight (liquid will drain out and yogurt will thicken).

Combine sesame seeds, salt, summer savory, cayenne and cumin in small bowl. Open cheesecloth at top. Using rubber spatula, transfer drained yogurt to bowl. Drizzle olive oil over. Sprinkle with sesame seed mixture. Place bowl in center of platter; surround with pita bread triangles and olives.

TOMATO FRITTERS

Whether they're made of ground meat, chickpeas, fish roe or vegetables, the fried appetizers called keftedes (literally "meatballs") are a favorite treat all over Greece. The vegetable ones on Santorini are considered to be the best-tasting because they are made with the delicious locally grown tomatoes, which have a firm texture and a distinctive flavor.

MAKES ABOUT 16

1⅓ cups diced seeded peeled
    plum tomatoes
⅔ cup finely diced zucchini
½ cup finely chopped onion
2 tablespoons chopped fresh mint
½ cup all-purpose flour
¾ teaspoon baking powder
½ teaspoon salt
½ teaspoon pepper
    Pinch of ground cinnamon

¼ cup (or more) olive oil

Combine diced tomatoes, zucchini, onion and mint in small bowl. Combine flour, baking powder, salt, pepper and cinnamon in medium bowl. Stir vegetable mixture into dry ingredients.

Heat ¼ cup olive oil in heavy large nonstick skillet over medium-high heat. Working in batches and adding more oil as necessary, drop batter by rounded tablespoonfuls into oil. Cook until golden brown, about 2 minutes per side. Transfer to paper towels and drain. Serve immediately.

Beverages

VERY SPECIAL CHAMPAGNE COCKTAIL

8 SERVINGS

2 ½-pint baskets fresh raspberries
2 tablespoons sugar
½ cup plus 2 tablespoons raspberry
    liqueur
¼ cup Cognac or other brandy

8 sugar cubes
1 750-ml bottle chilled brut
    Champagne
    Fresh raspberries
    Lemon peel strips

Combine 2 baskets raspberries and 2 tablespoons sugar in medium bowl. Mash berries lightly with fork. Let stand 15 minutes. Mix in liqueur and brandy. Pour into jar. Cover and let stand in dark cupboard 3 days. Strain raspberry mixture, pressing on solids with spoon to extract as much liquid as possible. (*Can be made 1 month ahead. Cover; chill.*)

Place 1 sugar cube in each of eight 6-ounce Champagne flutes. Pour 2 tablespoons raspberry mixture over each sugar cube. Pour Champagne over to fill glasses. Garnish each with raspberries and lemon peel.

Victorian "Eggnog"

The English used to call this version of the classic Christmas drink sack posset. *"Sack" referred to wines imported from Spain. "Posset"—from the Middle English* poshet *(of uncertain meaning)—is a hot drink made of sweetened, special milk and ale or wine.*

6 SERVINGS

2 cups whipping cream
1 cup half-and-half
6 large egg yolks
½ cup sugar
1 teaspoon ground nutmeg

6 tablespoons dry sherry
Additional ground nutmeg

Bring cream and half-and-half to simmer in large saucepan. Whisk yolks and sugar in large bowl to blend. Gradually whisk hot cream mixture into yolk mixture. Return mixture to same saucepan. Stir over medium-low heat until mixture thickens and leaves path on back of spoon when finger is drawn across, about 4 minutes (do not boil). Strain into bowl. Stir in nutmeg. Cool slightly. *(Can be made 1 day ahead. Cover and chill. If desired, rewarm over low heat, stirring occasionally, before continuing.)*

Divide warm or cold mixture among 6 cups or glasses. Stir 1 tablespoon sherry into each. Sprinkle additional nutmeg over each and serve.

Deluxe Kir Royale

4 SERVINGS

1¼ cups frozen unsweetened
    blackberries (about 5 ounces),
    thawed
4 tablespoons crème de cassis
    (preferably imported)
1 750-ml bottle chilled Champagne
    or other sparkling wine

Puree berries in processor. Press puree through sieve into small bowl; discard seeds. Spoon 1 tablespoon berry puree and 1 tablespoon crème de cassis into each of 4 Champagne flutes. Fill each flute with Champagne and serve.

Mint Tea

In Morocco, this is usually prepared in a special teapot. After the tea brews a bit, some is poured back and forth between the pot and an ornate tea glass, a procedure that is said to improve the brewing process. When ready, the tea is poured from a height of one to two feet into the small glasses.

6 SERVINGS

4 tea bags of green tea
1 cup packed fresh mint leaves
¼ cup sugar
3 cups boiling water

Place tea bags, fresh mint leaves and sugar in teapot. Pour 3 cups boiling water over and stir to dissolve sugar. Let steep 4 minutes and serve.

COFFEE TALK

These hot drinks may vary a bit from country to country (and even from coffeehouse to coffeehouse), but here are some useful guidelines:

- **Café au lait** is made by combining equal parts of coffee and heated milk. The two are poured simultaneously into a bowl or large cup.
- **Espresso** is brewed by forcing steam through finely ground dark-roasted coffee beans. It is extremely strong and therefore usually served in small cups.
- **Cappuccino** consists of equal parts of espresso, steamed milk and frothed milk (foam), poured into a cup in that order. Often it's topped with cinnamon or sweetened cocoa powder.
- **Caffè latte** begins with a shot of espresso (usually about one-third of the coffee cup). The cup is then filled up with steamed milk and topped with a thin layer of frothy milk.

IRISH COFFEE

4 SERVINGS

½ cup chilled whipping cream
2 tablespoons Cointreau or other orange liqueur
1 tablespoon powdered sugar

½ cup Irish cream liqueur
¼ cup Irish whiskey
¼ cup brandy
3 cups strong hot coffee
1 teaspoon grated orange peel

Combine cream, Cointreau and powdered sugar in medium bowl. Beat until medium-firm peaks form. (*Can be made 4 hours ahead. Cover and refrigerate.*)

Pour 2 tablespoons Irish cream liqueur, 1 tablespoon whiskey and 1 tablespoon brandy into each of four 8- to 10-ounce coffee mugs. Pour hot coffee over. Top each with dollop of whipped cream. Sprinkle with grated orange peel and serve immediately.

Soups & Salads

The world over, good cooks and enthusiastic eaters recognize the soul-restoring benefits of a slow-simmered soup or a fresh-from-the garden salad. You'll find great pleasure and comfort in such brimming bowlfuls as Indian Lemon Soup with Garbanzo Beans, Chinese Hot and Sour Soup or Dutch Farmer's Cheese Soup; and in such refreshing combinations as Asian Sesame Broccoli Salad, American Red Potato Salad with Dill or Greek Pasta Salad.

Soups

LEMON SOUP WITH GARBANZO BEANS

This light soup makes a lovely first course.

4 SERVINGS

6 cups canned chicken broth
1 15- to 16-ounce can garbanzo
    beans (chickpeas), rinsed,
    drained
6 garlic cloves, chopped
1½ teaspoons ground turmeric
⅛ teaspoon cumin seeds
2 large eggs
¼ cup fresh lemon juice
    Pinch of cayenne pepper
    Salt
2 tablespoons chopped fresh mint

Combine broth, garbanzo beans, garlic, turmeric and cumin seeds in large saucepan; bring to boil. Reduce heat and simmer soup 15 minutes. Whisk eggs and lemon juice in medium bowl until well blended. Gradually whisk 2 cups hot soup into egg mixture. Return egg mixture to saucepan; stir over medium-low heat until heated through, about 5 minutes (do not boil). Add cayenne pepper. Season with salt. Ladle soup into bowls. Sprinkle with mint and serve.

TALKING TURMERIC

Talk of turmeric brings up a basic question about human nature: Why do we like yellow food? For thousands of years turmeric has been coveted, partly for its taste and aroma but perhaps equally for its ability to bring a golden hue to anything edible. This Midas touch has won the spice a permanent place in the world's mustards, margarines, cheeses and liqueurs, many of which rely on turmeric to give them their sunny good looks.

But nowhere is turmeric more important than it is in curry. "For a spice blend to be called a curry powder," says Indian cookbook author Julie Sahni, "it must contain three core spices: coriander, turmeric and pepper." In the 1747 book *The Art of Cookery Made Plain and Easy,* English writer Hannah Glasse listed turmeric, ginger and pepper as the essential elements. And you'll be happy to know that for years, even the U.S. armed forces had a strict guideline regarding the composition of this Asian spice mix: Federal Military Specification EE-S-631J stipulated that 37 to 39 percent of the curry powder used in military mess halls had to be turmeric. Botanically, turmeric (*Curcuma longa*) is a rhizome, an underground root that has several short, blunt "fingers" and resembles ginger, which is in the same family. After being harvested, turmeric plants are boiled and peeled, then dried in the sun for several days before being ground to a powder, the form in which most turmeric is sold. Again, color plays a part: The yellower the turmeric, the better it is.

Turmeric originated in southern India, possibly along the Malabar Coast, where it grows wild. It is also harvested in China, Taiwan, Indonesia, Pakistan, Peru and the West Indies, but the United States buys virtually all of its supply from India, which produces some 225,000 metric tons a year, about 94 percent of the world's crop.

HOT AND SOUR SOUP WITH GINGER

4 SERVINGS

4 cups canned low-salt chicken broth

1½ ounces dried shiitake mushrooms

5 tablespoons rice vinegar

2 tablespoons cornstarch

1½ tablespoons Oriental sesame oil

3 tablespoons minced peeled fresh ginger

1 10.5-ounce package extra-firm or firm tofu, cut into ¼-inch dice

1 ounce bean thread noodles* or angel hair pasta, broken in half

1 tablespoon soy sauce

½ teaspoon dried crushed red pepper
Pinch of sugar

Combine broth and mushrooms in bowl. Let stand until mushrooms soften, about 20 minutes. Remove mushrooms from broth and squeeze dry over bowl with broth; reserve broth. Discard mushroom stems; thinly slice caps. Combine vinegar and cornstarch in small bowl; stir to blend.

Heat oil in large saucepan over high heat. Add ginger; sauté 30 seconds. Pour in reserved broth, leaving behind any sediment. Bring to boil. Add tofu, noodles, soy sauce, red pepper, sugar and mushrooms. Reduce heat to medium-low, cover and simmer 5 minutes. Add cornstarch mixture; stir until slightly thickened, about 1 minute.

*Clear dried noodles also known as cellophane or transparent noodles. Available at Asian markets and in the Asian section of some supermarkets

THE GINGER OF CHINA

Ginger root is actually a rhizome—a branching stem that when planted produces roots, leaves and flowers. Although its blossoms are lovely, this gnarled, knobby rhizome would not win any beauty contests. Thin, rough beige skin hides its pale, intense-tasting flesh. Fully matured ginger is fibrous and very pungent. Young ginger is milder, prettier and blushed with pink.

Fresh ginger in our markets today comes from Brazil, Costa Rica, Fiji, Hawaii, Indonesia and the Philippines, depending on the season. India and China supply most of the dried ginger.

The Chinese used ginger well before the time of Christ and introduced it wherever they traded or settled. Later, in Europe and North America, dried ginger became a major spice, and cupboards showed off fine porcelain ginger jars.

In China, ginger is regarded as a medicine as well as a seasoning. Its heating effect is said to relieve coughs and colds, stomach upsets, weak appetites and poor circulation. An ancient headache remedy involved roasting the root over an open fire and applying a few slices to the temples and forehead.

DUTCH FARMER'S CHEESE SOUP

A crouton topped with melted Gouda cheese is the delicious accent to an appealing meatless soup made of potatoes, cauliflower, carrots and onion.

6 SERVINGS

¼ cup (½ stick) butter
1½ pounds russet potatoes, peeled, diced
1 1½-pound cauliflower, trimmed, cut into florets
1 pound carrots, peeled, sliced
1 large onion, chopped
4 cups (or more) canned vegetable broth
Salt and pepper

6 1-inch-thick French bread slices
12 ounces Gouda cheese, wax removed, cheese sliced

Melt butter in heavy large Dutch oven over medium-high heat. Add potatoes, cauliflower, carrots and onion; sauté until onion is golden brown, about 7 minutes. Add 4 cups broth; bring to boil. Reduce heat; simmer until vegetables are tender, adding more broth if soup is too thick, about 30 minutes. Season to taste with salt and pepper. *(Can be prepared 1 day ahead. Cover and refrigerate. Bring to simmer before continuing.)*

Preheat broiler. Transfer soup to large broilerproof bowl or individual broilerproof soup bowls. Arrange bread slices atop soup. Place cheese slices over, covering bread completely. Broil 6 inches from heat source until cheese melts and is golden, watching closely to avoid burning, about 2 minutes. Serve immediately.

CHILLED BEET SOUP WITH DILL CREAM

4 SERVINGS

4 cups (or more) canned low-salt chicken broth
1 pound beets, peeled, chopped
1 cup chopped onion
¾ cup peeled chopped carrot
2 teaspoons chopped garlic
1 teaspoon sugar
Salt and pepper

2 tablespoons chopped fresh dill or 2 teaspoons dried dillweed
2 tablespoons chopped fresh chives or green onions
Sour cream

Combine 4 cups broth, beets, onion, carrot and garlic in medium saucepan. Bring to boil. Reduce heat to medium-low; cover and simmer until vegetables are very tender, about 35 minutes. Cool slightly. Puree in blender in batches until smooth. Transfer to bowl. Thin with additional broth if soup is too thick. Mix in sugar. Season with salt and pepper. Cover and chill until cold, at least 4 hours or overnight. *(Can be prepared 2 days ahead. Keep refrigerated.)*

Ladle soup into bowls. Sprinkle with dill and chives. Top with sour cream.

CILANTRO-LIME SOUP

4 SERVINGS

2 tablespoons olive oil
1 onion, chopped
2 garlic cloves, minced
1 tablespoon chili powder
2 skinless boneless chicken breast
  halves, cut into ¾-inch pieces
5 cups canned low-salt chicken
  broth
1 cup fresh or frozen corn kernels
1 cup chopped seeded tomatoes
½ bunch fresh cilantro sprigs, tied
  together with kitchen string

¼ cup chopped fresh cilantro
¼ cup fresh lime juice
  Salt and pepper
  Sour cream

Heat oil in heavy large saucepan over medium-high heat. Add onion and garlic; sauté until slightly softened, about 3 minutes. Add chili powder; stir 1 minute. Add chicken; stir 2 minutes.

Add broth, corn, tomatoes and ½ bunch cilantro sprigs to saucepan; bring to boil. Reduce heat and simmer until chicken is cooked through, about 10 minutes. Discard cilantro sprigs.

Can be made 1 day ahead. Chill. Bring to simmer before continuing.)

Add chopped cilantro and lime juice to soup. Season with salt and pepper. Garnish with sour cream.

SORTING OUT CILANTRO

Though its fragile leaves and wispy stems give cilantro a delicate look, the herb's peppery aroma and distinctive flavor—sharp and lemony with a hint of anise—add up to an assertive culinary personality. Cilantro has a cooling effect on the spicy elements of Mexican food and brings out the best of other key ingredients such as tomatoes, lemons and garlic. So it is only appropriate that Mexican cooks put it in everything from salsas and marinades to soups and salads.

But despite the unequivocal statement it makes in a variety of dishes, there is some confusion about what exactly cilantro is— probably because it goes by so many names in different parts of the world.

Cilantro is the Spanish word for the herb, but it is known elsewhere in Europe and beyond as *coriander*, from the Greek world *koris*, meaning "bed-bug." Apparently the plant shares a scent with the insect that in times past was an all-too-common houseguest. *Coriander* is the preferred name for cilantro in several parts of the United States, too, leading some American cooks to believe that the ground coriander seeds sold in the spice section at the grocery store can be used interchangeably with the fresh green leaves displayed in the produce department. Ground coriander does in fact come from the seeds of the same plant, and it does have a lovely floral aroma, but the flavors of coriander and cilantro are quite dissimilar.

Nor is *coriander* the only other name used to refer to the herb. In some parts of Asia, cilantro is called "Chinese parsley." Adding to the confusion, cilantro is strikingly similar in appearance to flat-leaf, or Italian, parsley. But, again, the taste of this and other parsley is completely different from that of cilantro.

VIETNAMESE BEEF SOUP

Called pho in Vietnam, this unusual soup is a wonderful party centerpiece dish for an informal gathering. Start out by supplying everyone with a large soup bowl and a ladle. Place the soup tureen in the middle of the table. Have each guest take a generous helping of noodles first, then some meat and broth. Each serving is topped off with shredded lettuce, sliced green onion and a squeeze of lemon juice.

8 SERVINGS

8 ounces bean thread noodles*

10 cups canned beef broth
2 medium onions, thickly sliced
4 ½-inch-thick slices fresh ginger
   (about 1¼ ounces)
2 tablespoons fish sauce (nam pla)*
3 large garlic cloves, halved
2 star anise*
1½ teaspoons whole cloves
1 pound flank steak, trimmed,
   thinly sliced crosswise

1 head romaine lettuce, thinly sliced
3 green onions, thinly sliced
   Lemon wedges

Bring large pot of water to boil. Remove from heat. Add noodles to pot; let stand until tender and pliable, about 15 minutes. Drain. Using scissors, cut noodles into 2-inch lengths. Transfer to bowl.

Combine beef broth, sliced onions, sliced ginger, fish sauce, garlic, star anise and whole cloves in heavy large Dutch oven and bring to boil. Reduce heat; simmer 30 minutes. Strain broth into large bowl; discard solids. *(Noodles and broth can be prepared 1 day ahead. Cover separately and refrigerate. Bring noodles to room temperature before continuing.)* Return beef broth to Dutch oven and bring to boil. Remove beef broth from heat. Mix steak slices into broth (the hot broth will cook steak slices).

Place noodles, soup, sliced lettuce, sliced green onions and lemon wedges in center of table. Spoon noodles, steak slices and broth into large soup bowls,

then top with generous amounts of sliced lettuce and green onions and squeeze in lemon juice.

*Bean thread noodles (clear dried noodles, also known as cellophane or transparent noodles), fish sauce (nam pla) and star anise are sold at Asian markets and in the Asian section of some supermarkets.

LEMON CHICKEN SOUP

4 MAIN-COURSE SERVINGS

9 cups canned low-salt chicken
   broth
3 celery stalks, chopped
2 large carrots, peeled, chopped
1 large onion, chopped
¾ cup long-grain white rice
1½ pounds skinless boneless chicken
   thighs, cut into bite-size pieces

3 large eggs, beaten to blend
½ cup fresh lemon juice
   Salt and pepper

Bring broth, celery, carrots and onion to boil in large pot. Add rice to soup and simmer until tender, about 30 minutes. Add chicken to soup and simmer until cooked through, about 10 minutes.

Beat eggs and lemon juice in small bowl until blended. Gradually add egg mixture to soup, stirring constantly until mixture forms ribbons. Simmer until flavors blend, about 3 minutes. Season soup to taste with salt and pepper

Salads

PASTA SALAD WITH SHRIMP AND OLIVES

For a nice picnic, pack up this salad (chill it well first), some bread and wine.

6 SERVINGS

¾ pound tomatoes, chopped
1 large red bell pepper, seeded, chopped
¼ pound feta cheese, crumbled

½ cup olive oil
½ cup chopped pitted black olives (preferably brine-cured)
¼ cup fresh lemon juice
2 tablespoons dry vermouth or dry white wine
1 tablespoon dried thyme
6 green onions, chopped
3 large garlic cloves, chopped
¾ pound linguine, freshly cooked
¾ pound cooked bay shrimp
   Salt and pepper

Mix first 10 ingredients in large bowl. Add linguine and shrimp and toss to blend. Season salad to taste with salt and pepper. (*Can be prepared 30 minutes ahead. Let stand at room temperature.*).

SESAME BROCCOLI SALAD

An easy side dish with a bit of Asian flavor.

6 SERVINGS

2 tablespoons soy sauce
2 tablespoons rice vinegar
2 tablespoons Oriental sesame oil
2 tablespoons honey
   Salt and pepper

12 cups broccoli florets (from 2 large bunches)

½ cup sesame seeds

Whisk soy sauce, vinegar, oil and honey in large bowl until blended. Season to taste with salt and pepper.

Steam broccoli florets until crisp-tender, about 5 minutes. Cool.

Stir sesame seeds in heavy large skillet over medium heat until golden, about 5 minutes. Transfer to small bowl; cool.

Mix broccoli and half of sesame seeds into dressing. Let marinate at room temperature at least 30 minutes or up to 2 hours, tossing occasionally. Transfer broccoli to platter. Pour dressing over. Sprinkle with remaining sesame seeds.

CUCUMBER, OLIVE, RADISH, ARUGULA AND FETA SALAD

Five distinctive Mediterranean ingredients harmonize beautifully in this takeoff on the classic Greek salad. Offer wedges of pita bread alongside.

6 SERVINGS

- 1 English hothouse cucumber, quartered lengthwise, cut crosswise into ½-inch-wide pieces
- 1 bunch radishes, quartered
- ½ pound Kalamata olives*
- 1 bunch (½ ounce) arugula, chopped
- 2 tablespoons olive oil
- 1 tablespoon fresh lemon juice
  Salt and pepper
- ⅓ pound feta cheese, cubed

Combine cucumber, radishes, olives and arugula in medium bowl. (*Can be made 6 hours ahead. Cover; chill.*) Add oil and lemon juice; toss to coat. Season with salt and pepper. Mix in cheese.

*Black, brine-cured Kalamata olives are available at Greek and Italian markets and some supermarkets.

IT'S THE PITS

There are two easy ways to pit an olive. For the first, place one olive on a work surface. Put the flat side of a large knife atop the olive, and firmly tap your fist on the knife to crack open the olive. Then simply remove the pit. Or you can buy an olive pitter, an implement that resembles a handheld hole punch. On one end is a small ring in which you place the olive, and on the opposing end is a metal prong. When the hinged handles are squeezed together, the metal prong pushes the pit out of the olive through the ring on the other side. This handy gadget can also be used to pit cherries. If you can't find it at your local kitchenware store, call Sur La Table at 800-243-0852.

JICAMA AND PINEAPPLE SALAD WITH CILANTRO VINAIGRETTE

Chopped cilantro in the dressing and whole leaves mixed with the spinach add a double dose of cilantro flavor to this salad.

4 SERVINGS

- ⅓ cup vegetable oil
- 3 tablespoons white wine vinegar
- 1 tablespoon minced shallot
- ¼ cup chopped fresh cilantro
- ¼ teaspoon ground cumin
  Salt and pepper
- 1 6-ounce package baby spinach, stems trimmed
- 1 small jicama, peeled, cut into 3-inch-long matchstick-size strips
- 1 cup cubed fresh pineapple
- ½ cup cilantro leaves

Whisk first 5 ingredients in small bowl to blend. Season with salt and pepper. Combine all remaining ingredients in large bowl. Toss with enough dressing to coat. Divide salad among 4 plates.

ORANGE, RED ONION AND WATERCRESS SALAD

A simple and refreshing way to start a Moroccan-inspired meal. The orange flower water is a flavoring extract produced from the flowers of the Seville orange. It's sold in liquor stores and in the liquor or specialty foods section of some supermarkets. It makes a lovely addition to this salad.

6 SERVINGS

⅓ cup extra-virgin olive oil
¼ cup orange juice
1 tablespoon red wine vinegar
1 tablespoon balsamic vinegar or
    red wine vinegar
1 teaspoon orange flower water
    (optional)
Salt and pepper

2 large bunches watercress,
    trimmed
4 oranges, peel and white pith
    removed, cut crosswise into

⅓-inch-thick rounds
1 small red onion, thinly sliced

Whisk first 4 ingredients in bowl. Add orange flower water, if desired. Season dressing to taste with salt and pepper. *(Can be prepared 1 day ahead. Cover; chill. Bring to room temperature before using.)*

Arrange watercress, oranges and onion on platter. Pour vinaigrette over.

A SPRINKLING OF ROSES OR ORANGES

Rose flower water and orange flower water are versatile ingredients that are used in many Mediterranean dishes. They can be splashed over orange slices, added to desserts, sprinkled into tea or even used to freshen the hands and face after a meal.

LENTIL AND CELERY ROOT SALAD

In the area around the town of Le Puy, farmers grow the famous lentilles vertes, or green lentils, renowned for their deep color (which turns brown during cooking) and rich texture. An integral part of classic Auvergnat cuisine, they show up in traditional dishes such as petit salé aux lentilles, or salt pork with lentils. Here they are combined with celery root and blue cheese in a robust salad. It's best with Bleu d'Auvergne, a regional blue available at specialty cheese stores.

4 SERVINGS

1 1- to 1¼-pound celery root
    (celeriac)

1 cup French green lentils

6 tablespoons olive oil
3 tablespoons white wine vinegar
1½ teaspoons minced garlic
1 teaspoon minced fresh rosemary

Large pinch of ground nutmeg
Salt and pepper
½ cup crumbled blue cheese

Cook celery root in pot of boiling salted water until tender, about 45 minutes. Drain, cool and peel. Cut enough of root into ¼-inch cubes to yield 1½ cups.

Cook lentils in pot of boiling salted water until just tender but still firm to bite, about 20 minutes. Drain; cool.

Whisk oil, vinegar, garlic, rosemary and nutmeg to blend in small bowl. Season with salt and pepper; add cheese.

Mix celery root, lentils and dressing in bowl. (*Can be made 4 hours ahead. Let stand at room temperature. Toss occasionally.*)

INDIA

POTATO, CUCUMBER AND TOMATO RAITA

Raita is a yogurt salad, an integral—and cool—part of an Indian meal. It can be prepared with raw and/or cooked vegetables (we use both here) or with fruit.

6 SERVINGS

4 large red-skinned potatoes, peeled, cut into ½-inch cubes

2 tablespoons vegetable oil
1 large onion, finely chopped
2 jalapeño chilies, seeded, chopped
1 tablespoon mustard seeds
1 tablespoon cumin seeds
3 cups low-fat (do not use nonfat) plain yogurt
1 English hothouse cucumber, cut into ½-inch cubes
3 large tomatoes, seeded, cut into ½-inch pieces
Salt and pepper
Fresh cilantro leaves

Cook potatoes in large pot of boiling salted water until just tender, about 8 minutes. Drain potatoes well. Transfer potatoes to large bowl and cool.

Heat vegetable oil in heavy medium skillet over high heat. Add chopped onion and stir until beginning to brown, about 4 minutes. Add chopped jalapeño chilies and stir until beginning to soften, about 1 minute. Add mustard seeds and cumin seeds and stir until aromatic, about 30 seconds. Immediately pour onion mixture over potatoes and stir to coat. Mix in low-fat yogurt, cucumber and tomatoes. Season raita to taste with salt and pepper. Cover tightly and refrigerate until well chilled, at least 2 hours. (*Raita can be prepared up to 6 hours ahead. Keep refrigerated.*) Garnish raita with fresh cilantro leaves and serve.

Chinese Noodle and Chicken Salad

Store-bought roasted chicken makes this rendition of a popular salad a snap to prepare. It's made spicy by combining chilies with linguine, green onions, snow peas, cilantro and a peanut dressing.

20 SERVINGS

SALAD

2 pounds linguine
¼ cup Oriental sesame oil
2 2½-pound roasted chickens, skinned, boned, shredded
4 bunches green onions, sliced
2 bunches fresh cilantro, chopped
4 jalapeño chilies, seeded, deveined, minced

1¼ pounds snow peas, stringed, thinly sliced lengthwise

DRESSING

1 cup soy sauce
½ cup creamy peanut butter (do not use old-fashioned style or freshly ground)
½ cup rice vinegar
½ cup Oriental sesame oil
2 tablespoons sugar

Napa cabbage leaves

FOR SALAD: Cook linguine in large pot of boiling salted water until just tender but still firm to bite. Drain. Rinse with cold water to cool; drain well. Transfer to large bowl. Add sesame oil; toss to blend. Mix in chicken, onions, cilantro and chilies.

Cook snow peas in medium saucepan of boiling salted water until just crisp-tender, about 1 minute. Drain. Rinse with cold water to cool; drain well. Mix into salad.

FOR DRESSING: Combine soy sauce, peanut butter, vinegar, sesame oil and sugar in processor; blend until smooth.

Pour dressing over salad and mix with hands to blend well. (*Can be prepared 1 day ahead. Cover and refrigerate.*) Line large platter with Napa cabbage leaves. Mound salad over and serve.

Lentil, Garbanzo Bean and Tomato Salad

4 SERVINGS

2½ cups water
1 cup lentils
2 large carrots, peeled, diced
1 bay leaf

1 15- to 16-ounce can garbanzo beans (chickpeas), rinsed, drained
½ basket cherry tomatoes, halved
1 cup chopped fresh parsley
5 green onions, chopped
4½ tablespoons olive oil
2 tablespoons plus 1 teaspoon fresh lemon juice
Salt and pepper

Combine 2½ cups water, lentils, diced carrots and bay leaf in heavy medium saucepan. Bring to boil. Reduce heat, cover and simmer until lentils are just tender, about 25 minutes. Drain; transfer to large bowl. Cool.

Mix all remaining ingredients into lentils. Season to taste with salt and pepper. (Can be prepared 4 hours ahead. Cover and refrigerate.)

KOHLRABI COLESLAW WITH PAPRIKA DRESSING

4 SERVINGS

3 tablespoons white wine vinegar
1 tablespoon sweet Hungarian paprika
½ cup olive oil
2 teaspoons purchased cream-style white horseradish
½ teaspoon sugar
Salt and pepper

2 large kohlrabi (leafy tops reserved), trimmed, peeled, cut into large pieces

1 large carrot, peeled, cut into 2-inch lengths

Combine vinegar and paprika in bowl. Whisk in oil. Mix in horseradish and sugar. Season with salt and pepper.

Using medium shredding disk, shred kohlrabi and carrot in processor. Transfer vegetables to bowl. Thinly slice enough kohlrabi leaves to make 1 cup; add to bowl. Toss with dressing. Let stand at least 30 minutes before serving.

CHICKEN SALAD WITH GREENS, ROASTED POTATOES AND SHALLOTS

Skinless, boneless chicken breasts and mixed baby greens—the kind sold pre-washed and ready to eat—have become indispensable to the modern, health-conscious cook on the go. Here they're paired in a salad that's sure to please. (You could also pick up roasted chicken breasts at a local take-out shop if you're really in a rush.)

4 SERVINGS

ROASTED VEGETABLES

2 large russet potatoes, cut into ½-inch cubes
8 large shallots, cut lengthwise into ¼-inch-thick slices
3 tablespoons olive oil
Salt and pepper

CHICKEN AND SALAD

12 cups mixed baby greens (about 8 ounces)
½ cup all-purpose flour
4 skinless boneless chicken breast halves
1 tablespoon olive oil

Shallot and Mustard Vinaigrette (see recipe)

FOR ROASTED VEGETABLES: Preheat oven to 450°F. Combine all ingredients in baking pan. Season with salt and pepper. Stir to coat. Bake until golden and cooked through, stirring occasionally, about 30 minutes.

FOR CHICKEN AND SALAD: Place greens in large bowl and chill. Place flour in shallow dish. Season with salt and pepper. Coat chicken with flour. Heat oil in heavy large skillet over medium-high heat. Add chicken and cook until cooked through, about 4 minutes per side.

Transfer to work surface.

Add roasted vegetables to greens. Add ¼ cup vinaigrette and toss to coat. Divide among plates. Slice chicken on diagonal. Fan chicken atop greens. Drizzle with remaining vinaigrette and serve.

SHALLOT AND MUSTARD VINAIGRETTE

MAKES ABOUT ½ CUP

1 large shallot, minced
1 tablespoon Dijon mustard
2 tablespoons balsamic vinegar
⅓ cup plus 2 tablespoons olive oil
1½ tablespoons chopped fresh thyme
  or 1½ teaspoons dried
  Salt and pepper

Combine minced shallot and Dijon mustard in small bowl. Whisk in balsamic vinegar. Gradually whisk in olive oil. Add thyme. Season vinaigrette to taste with salt and pepper. *(Can be prepared 1 day ahead. Cover and refrigerate. Bring to room temperature before using.)*

WARM CHICKEN SALAD WITH SOY-GINGER DRESSING

4 APPETIZER OR 2 MAIN-COURSE SERVINGS

3 tablespoons sake
3 tablespoons soy sauce
1 egg, beaten to blend
2¼ teaspoons Oriental sesame oil
  Pepper
2 skinless boneless chicken breast
  halves, cut crosswise into strips

¼ cup canned low-salt chicken broth
1½ tablespoons chili sauce
  (such as Heinz)
1 tablespoon minced green onion
1 tablespoon fresh lemon juice
1 tablespoon sugar
1 teaspoon minced peeled fresh
  ginger
1 small head iceberg lettuce,
  shredded
  Cornstarch
2 tablespoons peanut oil

Combine sake, 1 tablespoon soy sauce, egg and 2 teaspoons sesame oil in shallow dish. Season with pepper. Add chicken and turn to coat. Cover and refrigerate 15 minutes to 1 hour.

Combine broth, chili sauce, green onion, lemon juice, sugar, ginger, 2 tablespoons soy sauce and ¼ teaspoon sesame oil in small bowl. Set dressing aside. Arrange lettuce on platter.

Drain chicken. Coat lightly with cornstarch. Heat peanut oil in heavy large skillet over high heat. Add chicken and fry until just cooked through, about 3 minutes. Using slotted spoon, transfer chicken to lettuce-lined platter. Drizzle with dressing and serve.

ROAST BEEF SALAD WITH CABBAGE AND HORSERADISH

2 MAIN-COURSE SERVINGS

3 tablespoons prepared white horseradish
2 tablespoons plus 1 teaspoon balsamic vinegar
2¼ teaspoons Dijon mustard
6 tablespoons olive oil

4 cups finely shredded red cabbage

6 ounces thinly sliced roast beef, cut crosswise into strips
1 cup coarsely grated peeled celery root (celeriac)
½ cup thinly sliced red onion
½ cup crumbled Roquefort cheese
Salt and pepper
Chopped fresh parsley

Whisk first 3 ingredients in small bowl to blend. Gradually whisk in 5 tablespoons olive oil.

Heat remaining 1 tablespoon oil in large nonstick skillet over medium-high heat. Add cabbage and sauté just until wilted, about 3 minutes. Transfer to large bowl; cool completely.

Mix roast beef, celery root, onion, cheese and dressing into cabbage. Season with salt and pepper. Divide salad between 2 plates. Sprinkle with parsley.

ITALIAN SAUSAGE PASTA SALAD

Accompany this robust salad with crusty bread and serve grapes for dessert.

6 TO 8 SERVINGS

¾ pound sweet Italian sausages, casings removed
2 tablespoons olive oil
1 cup chopped onion
4 large garlic cloves, chopped
3 cups broccoli florets
1 medium zucchini, cut into ¾-inch pieces
¼ cup dry white wine
5 large plum tomatoes, seeded, diced
1 pound rotini or fusilli pasta, freshly cooked
1 cup grated Parmesan cheese
½ cup drained chopped black olives
½ cup (about) purchased Parmesan cheese salad dressing
Salt and pepper

Sauté sausage in heavy large skillet over medium heat until cooked through, breaking up with spoon, about 6 minutes. Using slotted spoon, transfer sausage to paper towels. Pour off drippings; add oil to same skillet. Add onion and garlic; sauté until translucent, about 5 minutes. Add broccoli, zucchini and wine; sauté until vegetables are just tender, about 4 minutes. Add sausage and tomatoes; toss until heated through, about 2 minutes. Transfer to large bowl. Add pasta, cheese, olives and enough dressing to coat. Season with salt and pepper.

RED POTATO SALAD WITH DILL

6 SERVINGS

2 pounds red-skinned potatoes,
   cut into bite-size pieces
1 red bell pepper, chopped
1 onion, chopped
6 tablespoons mayonnaise
6 tablespoons plain yogurt
¼ cup chopped fresh dill
1 tablespoon Dijon mustard
1 tablespoon balsamic vinegar
1 tablespoon prepared white
   horseradish

Cook potatoes in large pot of boiling salted water until tender, about 10 minutes. Drain; cool slightly. Combine potatoes, bell pepper and onion in large bowl. Whisk mayonnaise and all remaining ingredients in medium bowl. Pour half of dressing over warm potato mixture; toss to coat. Let stand 1 hour. (*Can be made*

1 day ahead. Cover salad and remaining dressing separately; chill. Bring to room temperature before continuing.)

Toss potato salad with remaining dressing and serve.

ASIAN NOODLE SALAD WITH CHILIES AND PEANUTS

6 SERVINGS

1 pound dried soba noodles or
   spaghetti
¼ cup Oriental sesame oil
¼ cup soy sauce
2 tablespoons sugar
1½ tablespoons balsamic vinegar
   or red wine vinegar
2 teaspoons salt
1 cup chopped fresh cilantro
8 green onions, thinly sliced
2 to 3 red or green jalapeño chilies,
   seeded, veins removed, minced
   (about 2 tablespoons)
1½ cups lightly salted dry-roasted
   peanuts, coarsely chopped
   (about 7½ ounces)

Cook noodles in large pot of rapidly boiling salted water until just tender but still firm to bite, stirring occasionally. Drain. Rinse noodles with cold water until cool. Drain well. Transfer to large bowl. Combine sesame oil, soy sauce, sugar, vinegar and salt in small bowl. Stir to dissolve sugar. Add to noodles. Add chopped fresh cilantro, green onions and jalapeño chilies and mix well. (*Salad can be prepared 1 day ahead. Cover and refrigerate.*) Sprinkle chopped peanuts over salad and serve.

BEET AND POTATO SALAD
4 SERVINGS

3 medium-size red-skinned
  potatoes (about ¾ pound)
3 beets
6 tablespoons white distilled vinegar
4½ tablespoons olive oil
4 teaspoons ground coriander
  Salt and pepper

Cook potatoes and beets in separate medium pots of boiling salted water until tender, about 30 minutes for potatoes and 35 minutes for beets. Drain; cool slightly. Peel vegetables and thinly slice into rounds. Whisk vinegar, oil and coriander in medium bowl. Season generously with salt and pepper. Add vegetables; toss gently to coat. (*Can be made 2 hours ahead. Let stand at room temperature.*)

SPICY EGGPLANT, PEPPER AND TOMATO SALAD
6 SERVINGS

1 1-pound eggplant, cut into ¾-inch
  pieces
  Salt

1 large red bell pepper
1 large green bell pepper

2 medium zucchini, cut into ¾-inch
  pieces
1 cup water
¼ cup olive oil
2 garlic cloves, crushed
½ teaspoon dried crushed red pepper
2 large plum tomatoes, peeled,
  seeded, diced

12 Kalamata olives or other black,
  brine-cured olives, pitted
  Salt and pepper
  Warm pita bread, cut into triangles

Place eggplant in colander. Sprinkle with salt. Let stand 30 minutes to drain.

Char bell peppers over gas flame or under broiler until blackened on all sides. Wrap in paper bag and let stand 15 minutes. Peel, seed and stem peppers. Cut into ½-inch pieces.

Pat eggplant dry. Combine eggplant, zucchini, water, oil, garlic and dried red pepper in heavy medium saucepan. Bring to simmer over medium heat. Add tomatoes and cook until vegetables are almost tender, stirring occasionally, about 15 minutes. Stir in roasted bell peppers and simmer until vegetables are very tender and almost all liquid has evaporated, about 35 minutes.

Stir olives into vegetable mixture. Season with salt and pepper. Cool to room temperature. (*Can be made 2 days ahead; chill. Bring to room temperature before serving.*) Serve with pita bread.

Main Courses

Wherever you travel, whatever language is spoken, one common question is heard in homes everywhere come evening: "What's for dinner?" This widely ranging chapter provides a delightfully polyglot answer, including dishes like Chinese Ginger-Garlic Shrimp, Middle Eastern Baked Whitefish, Sri Lankan Chicken Curry, Hungarian Chicken Paprikás, French Beef Bourguignon, German Roast Pork with Cabbage and Caraway, Mediterranean Vegetable Couscous and Mexican Cheese Enchiladas.

Seafood

Sea Bass, Languedoc Style

The pink-skinned garlic from the village of Lautrec outside the city of Albi is highly regarded throughout France. The most pungent of all varieties, it is reputed to keep for a year from the time it is harvested. Garlic is shown off deliciously in this simple—and typical—main course.

2 SERVINGS

4 tablespoons extra-virgin olive oil
2 8-ounce sea bass fillets or tuna steaks (1 inch thick)
    Salt and pepper
12 large garlic cloves, sliced
8 fresh thyme sprigs (left whole)
3 tablespoons fresh lemon juice
    Chopped fresh chives or green onion tops

Heat 2 tablespoons oil in heavy large nonstick skillet over medium-high heat. Season fish with salt and pepper. Add to skillet and sauté until just cooked through, turning occasionally, about 8 minutes. Transfer fish to plates. Reduce heat to medium-low. Add remaining 2 tablespoons oil, garlic and thyme and cook until garlic is golden brown, stirring occasionally, about 4 minutes. Add lemon juice and simmer until liquid thickens slightly, about 1 minute. Season to taste with salt. Spoon sauce, garlic and thyme over fish. Sprinkle with chives and serve.

Super-Hot Shrimp Creole

Serve over rice—and keep a fire extinguisher nearby. Start with only 2 teaspoons Cajun seasoning and ½ teaspoon dried crushed red pepper flakes; then adjust as the mixture cooks.

4 SERVINGS

2 tablespoons vegetable oil
6 ounces fresh mushrooms, chopped (about 2 cups)
1 medium onion, chopped
1 green bell pepper, chopped
8 large garlic cloves, chopped
2 teaspoons to 2 tablespoons Cajun (Creole) seasoning for seafood
½ to 1½ teaspoons dried crushed red pepper
1 28-ounce can crushed tomatoes with added puree
1 14½-ounce can stewed tomatoes (preferably Cajun style)
1 pound uncooked shrimp, shelled, deveined

Heat oil in heavy large skillet over medium heat. Add mushrooms, onion, green pepper and garlic and sauté until onion is translucent, about 5 minutes. Add Cajun seasoning and crushed red pepper and stir 1 minute. Mix in crushed tomatoes and stewed tomatoes with their juices; simmer until sauce is thick, stirring occasionally, about 15 minutes. Add shrimp and simmer until just cooked through, about 5 minutes.

GINGER-GARLIC SHRIMP

You can add some diced red bell pepper to give this full-flavored dish a splash of color.

4 SERVINGS

1 pound uncooked shrimp, peeled, deveined
1 tablespoon Oriental sesame oil or vegetable oil
1 tablespoon minced garlic
1 tablespoon minced fresh ginger
¼ teaspoon dried crushed red pepper
3 tablespoons soy sauce

2 teaspoons cornstarch
½ cup canned low-salt chicken broth
¼ cup rice vinegar
2 tablespoons sugar

6 green onions, cut into ½-inch pieces
1 cup snow peas
Cooked rice

Combine first 5 ingredients in medium bowl. Add 1 tablespoon soy sauce and toss to coat. Let stand 15 minutes.

Meanwhile, place cornstarch in small bowl. Gradually add broth, stirring until cornstarch dissolves. Mix in vinegar, sugar and 2 tablespoons soy sauce.

Heat wok or heavy large skillet over high heat. Add shrimp mixture, green onions and snow peas and stir-fry until shrimp are pink and almost cooked through, about 3 minutes. Add cornstarch mixture; stir until sauce thickens, about 1 minute. Serve with rice.

TERIYAKI SALMON WITH BOK CHOY AND BABY CORN

Lemongrass and ginger bring new depth to the delicious glaze on the fish.

6 SERVINGS

1 cup sake
¾ cup soy sauce
¼ cup sugar
5 quarter-size slices fresh ginger
2 lemongrass stalks, sliced, or peel from ½ lemon, cut into ½-inch-wide strips

6 6-ounce salmon fillets

2 tablespoons vegetable oil
4 quarter-size slices fresh ginger, peeled, minced
1 2-pound head bok choy, cut into ¾-inch-thick slices, white and green parts separated
1 15-ounce can baby corn, drained, halved lengthwise
Salt
½ cup thinly sliced fresh basil

Combine sake, soy sauce, sugar, ginger slices and lemongrass in heavy small saucepan. Bring to simmer, stirring to dissolve sugar. Simmer teriyaki glaze 10 minutes to blend flavors. (*Can be prepared 1 day ahead. Cover and store at room temperature.*) Strain.

Preheat broiler. Arrange salmon

skin side down on broiler pan. Reserve 3 tablespoons teriyaki glaze for vegetables. Brush salmon generously with some of remaining glaze. Broil without turning until cooked through, about 8 minutes, brushing with glaze every 2 minutes.

Meanwhile, heat 2 tablespoons vegetable oil in heavy large skillet over high heat. Add minced ginger and stir-fry until aromatic, about 30 seconds. Add white part of bok choy and stir-fry until beginning to soften, about 3 minutes. Add green part of bok choy and baby corn and sprinkle with salt. Stir-fry until bok choy is wilted and corn is heated through, about 2 minutes. Add sliced fresh basil and reserved 3 tablespoons teriyaki glaze and stir to coat.

Place salmon on plates. Spoon vegetables alongside and serve.

CLAMS IN SPICY COCONUT-LIME BROTH

Complement this fragrant dish with Asian noodles or steamed rice.

4 SERVINGS

1 tablespoon vegetable oil
5 large shallots, chopped
1 tablespoon chopped peeled fresh ginger
1 teaspoon ground turmeric
¼ teaspoon cumin seeds
2 pounds littleneck clams, scrubbed
1½ cups bottled clam juice
1 cup canned unsweetened coconut milk*
1 cup diced canned tomatoes with juices
1 jalapeño chili, seeded, chopped
1 teaspoon grated lime peel
3 tablespoons fresh lime juice
Salt and pepper
2 green onions, sliced

Heat 1 tablespoon vegetable oil in large Dutch oven over medium heat. Add chopped shallots and sauté until tender, about 3 minutes. Add 1 tablespoon ginger, 1 teaspoon turmeric and ¼ teaspoon cumin and stir 1 minute. Add clams, clam juice, coconut milk, tomatoes with their juices, jalapeño and lime peel and bring to boil. Cover and cook until clams open, about 7 minutes (discard any that do not open). Stir in lime juice. Season to taste with salt and pepper. Transfer clams and sauce to bowl; sprinkle with green onions and serve.

Coconut milk is available at Indian, Southeast Asian and Latin American markets and many supermarkets.

BAKED WHITEFISH WITH TOMATOES AND GARLIC

4 SERVINGS

1 large bunch cilantro, chopped
3 large garlic cloves, chopped

3 tomatoes, sliced
4 5- to 6-ounce whitefish or sea
  bass fillets
¼ cup olive oil
1 tablespoon paprika
1 teaspoon instant chicken bouillon
  granules
½ teaspoon ground cumin
½ teaspoon ground turmeric
½ teaspoon ground pepper
3 cups (about) water

Spread cilantro evenly over bottom of heavy Dutch oven. Sprinkle with garlic; arrange tomatoes over. Set fish atop tomatoes. Whisk oil, paprika, bouillon granules, cumin, turmeric and pepper to blend in small bowl. Pour over fish. Add enough water to pot to reach bottom of fish. Bring water to boil over high heat. Cover pot, reduce heat to medium-low and simmer until fish is just cooked through, about 10 minutes.

Using large spatula, transfer fish and vegetables to platter. Spoon some cooking liquid over and serve.

OLIVE OIL ON THE LINE

Olive oil, a fundamental ingredient in Mediterranean cooking is a healthful alternative to butter and other oils. It can be used in place of vegetable oil for frying or sautéing, and its distinct aroma and flavor make it delicious on salads and breads. A big plus is that olive oil is about 70 percent *mono*unsaturated fat. This kind of fat is believed to be effective in raising the good blood cholesterol level and lowering the bad. But while monounsaturated fat might help your cholesterol count, remember that fat is fat, so olive oil won't make you skinny: If you're watching your weight, limit your intake of *all* fats.

GRILLED SPICED SEA BASS WITH FRESH MANGO SALSA

Mango, red onion, jalapeños and cilantro combine to make a zippy complement to grilled sea bass.

6 SERVINGS

SALSA
2 mangoes, peeled, pitted, chopped
1 small red onion, chopped
1 cup chopped fresh cilantro
  (about 1 large bunch)
2 green jalapeño chilies, seeded,
  minced
¼ cup fresh lime juice
2 tablespoons olive oil
  Salt and pepper

FISH
6 6-ounce sea bass fillets
  (about 1 inch thick)
  Olive oil
  Fresh lime juice
  Chili powder

FOR SALSA: Combine all ingredients in bowl. Season with salt and pepper.

FOR FISH: Place fish in single layer in baking dish. Brush both sides with oil and lime juice. Sprinkle with chili powder. *(Fish and salsa can be prepared 4 hours ahead. Cover separately and chill.)*

Prepare barbecue (medium-high heat) or preheat broiler. Sprinkle fish with salt and grill or broil until just cooked through, about 4 minutes per side. Transfer to plates. Serve with salsa.

PUT ON SOME SALSA

Looking to add the *picante* touch to everything from crudités to grilled fish? One of the three zesty sauces from Paula's Salsa Nova will do the trick. Choose from a Mild Cilantro & Walnut, Hot Sweet Red Jalapeño Pepper and Very Hot Jalapeño & Cilantro.

Chicken

SRI LANKA

CHICKEN CURRY

6 SERVINGS

⅔ cup chopped onion
5 large garlic cloves
2 tablespoons chopped peeled fresh ginger
1 tablespoon curry powder
1 tablespoon ground cinnamon
¾ teaspoon dried crushed red pepper
½ cup chopped fresh cilantro
12 chicken thighs

2 tablespoons vegetable oil
2 cups canned unsweetened coconut milk*
1 cup canned chicken broth
½ teaspoon turmeric
Salt
Freshly cooked rice

Blend first 6 ingredients and ¼ cup cilantro in processor to paste, stopping frequently to scrape down sides of bowl. Rub paste over chicken.

Heat oil in heavy large skillet over medium-high heat. Add chicken and brown on all sides, about 6 minutes. Add coconut milk, broth and turmeric. Reduce heat, cover and simmer until chicken is cooked through, turning once, about 30 minutes. Transfer chicken to plate. Boil liquid in skillet until reduced to sauce consistency, about 4 minutes. Season with salt. Return chicken to skillet; heat through. Sprinkle with remaining ¼ cup cilantro. Serve over rice.

Available at Indian, Southeast Asian or Latin American markets and some supermarkets. If unavailable, substitute 2 cups half-and-half mixed with 1 teaspoon imitation coconut extract.

SRI LANKA'S CINNAMON

In the wild, cinnamon trees can grow as tall as 50 feet. In contrast, cultivated trees are kept pruned to eight-foot-tall bushes. This keeps the shoots narrow and easily accessible, and the bark thin and tender. At harvest time (generally following the rainy season, when the tree's aromatic oils are at their peak), the straightest two-year-old shoots are cut and taken to a processing center.

The outer bark is carefully scraped away, and the paper-thin inner bark is peeled off. This inner bark rolls naturally into quills, and as it dries, smaller pieces are fitted into larger ones until a 3½-foot "pipe" is formed. These rolled quills, or pipes, are eventually tied into hundred-pound bundles for shipping.

While Sri Lanka exports an average of about seven thousand tons of cinnamon per year, little of that ever reaches the United States. Americans, it seems, have developed a taste for the more pungent type of cinnamon known as cassia. Grown in both China and Indonesia, this reddish-brown bark is what's commonly found in powdered and stick forms on the spice shelves of most supermarkets, where labels simply say cinnamon.

Cassia cinnamon will certainly taste delicious; but if you wish to sample true cinnamon, you may have to purchase it from a spice shop. One excellent source is Penzeys' Spice House in Milwaukee.

PROVENÇAL SAUTÉED CHICKEN
4 SERVINGS

1 4½-pound chicken, cut into 8 pieces
Salt and pepper
3 tablespoons olive oil
1 cup chopped salt pork (about 2½ ounces)
1 cup chopped onion
1 28-ounce can diced peeled tomatoes with juices
1 14½-ounce can low-salt chicken broth
¾ cup dry white wine
6 fresh thyme sprigs or 1 tablespoon dried
3 large garlic cloves, minced
2 bay leaves

1 cup drained Niçoise olives
½ cup sliced fresh basil

Season chicken with salt and pepper. Heat oil in heavy large Dutch oven over medium-high heat. Working in batches, add chicken and brown on all sides, about 5 minutes per batch. Transfer chicken to plate. Pour off all but 2 tablespoons fat from Dutch oven. Add salt pork; sauté until golden, about 5 minutes. Add onion and sauté until almost tender and golden, about 6 minutes. Add tomatoes with their juices, broth, wine, thyme, garlic and bay leaves and bring to boil. Return chicken to Dutch oven. Cover and simmer until chicken is cooked through, about 20 minutes.

Transfer chicken to large bowl. Add olives to Dutch oven and boil until mixture is reduced to 3 cups, about 25 minutes. Mix in basil. Return chicken to Dutch oven and stir until heated through, about 3 minutes. Transfer chicken to shallow serving bowl. Spoon sauce over and serve.

CHICKEN WITH INDIAN APRICOT SAUCE

4 SERVINGS

8 whole cardamom pods
3 shallots, sliced
1 2-inch piece fresh ginger, peeled, sliced
1 teaspoon (generous) fennel seeds
1 teaspoon (generous) cumin seeds
½ teaspoon whole black peppercorns
¾ cup canned chicken broth

1 3½- to 4-pound chicken, skinned
2½ tablespoons fresh lemon juice
2 teaspoons paprika
Salt and pepper
4 tablespoons (½ stick) butter

1½ pounds apricots, pitted, sliced
2 tablespoons (about) sugar

Steamed rice
1 tablespoon minced fresh cilantro
Additional sliced apricots

Crush cardamom with flat side of knife; discard shells. Place seeds in blender. Add shallots, ginger, fennel, cumin and peppercorns. Puree until paste forms. Add ¼ cup broth; process until smooth. (*Spice paste can be made 1 day ahead; chill.*)

Preheat oven to 400°F. Rub chicken with lemon juice and paprika; season with salt and pepper. Tie chicken legs together. Melt 2 tablespoons butter in heavy large skillet over medium heat. Add chicken to skillet and brown on all sides, about 15 minutes. Transfer chicken to heavy Dutch oven just large enough to accommodate chicken snugly.

Melt 2 tablespoons butter in same skillet over medium heat. Add 1½ pounds apricots; sauté until very tender, about 5 minutes. Reduce heat to low. Stir in spice paste; simmer 5 minutes. Mix in ½ cup broth and sugar to taste. Season with salt. Pour apricot mixture over chicken. Cover tightly; roast in oven until juices run clear when thigh is pierced in thickest part, about 45 minutes.

Cut chicken into pieces. Place rice on platter. Top with chicken and sauce. Sprinkle with cilantro; garnish with additional apricot slices.

CHICKEN PAPRIKÁS

Spoon this over egg noodles that have been tossed with butter and poppy seeds.

4 SERVINGS

- 4 large boneless chicken breast halves (about 1⅔ pounds)
  Salt and pepper
  All-purpose flour
- 3 tablespoons olive oil
- 2 red, yellow or green bell peppers, cut into strips
- 1 medium onion, sliced
- 4 large garlic cloves, chopped
- 5 teaspoons sweet Hungarian paprika
- ¼ teaspoon hot Hungarian paprika
- 1¼ cups canned chicken broth
- 4 large canned Italian plum tomatoes, chopped, drained
- 1 tablespoon tomato paste

Season chicken with salt and pepper. Coat with flour, shaking off excess. Heat oil in heavy large skillet over high heat. Add chicken to skillet and sauté until brown and crisp, about 4 minutes per side. Transfer chicken to plate. Add bell peppers, onion and garlic to skillet and sauté 5 minutes. Reduce heat to low. Add both paprikas and stir 2 minutes. Mix in broth, tomatoes and tomato paste. Return chicken to skillet. Bring liquids to simmer. Cover skillet and simmer gently until chicken is just cooked through, about 8 minutes.

Transfer chicken to platter; keep warm. Increase heat to high and boil until sauce coats spoon thickly, about 8 minutes. Season with salt and pepper. Spoon sauce over chicken.

GARLIC CHICKEN

4 SERVINGS

- ½ cup distilled white vinegar
- ½ cup canned low-salt chicken broth
- 10 large garlic cloves, chopped
- 2½ tablespoons soy sauce
- ¼ teaspoon ground pepper
- 4 skinless boneless chicken breast halves
- 2 teaspoons onion-herb seasoning mix (such as Mrs. Dash)
- 1 tablespoon Oriental sesame oil
- 3 large bay leaves
  Salt
  Cooked white rice

Whisk vinegar, chicken broth, garlic, soy sauce and pepper in small bowl to blend. Season chicken breast halves on both sides with seasoning mix. Heat oil in heavy large skillet over medium-high heat. Add chicken and sauté until golden, about 4 minutes per side. Pour vinegar mixture over chicken. Add bay leaves. Reduce heat to low, cover skillet and simmer until chicken is just cooked through, about 10 minutes. Using tongs, transfer chicken to plate. Boil pan juices 2 minutes. Season to taste with salt. Spoon over chicken, discarding bay leaves. Serve with rice.

CHICKEN WITH RAISINS AND LEMON
4 SERVINGS

1 3½-pound chicken, cut into
  8 pieces
2 tablespoons olive oil
2 large russet potatoes, peeled,
  cut into 1½-inch chunks
2 teaspoons minced garlic
1½ teaspoons ground turmeric
  Salt and pepper
1 large lemon, peel and white pith
  cut away, very thinly sliced
½ cup raisins
3½ cups (about) canned low-salt
  chicken broth
2 tablespoons fresh lemon juice

Arrange chicken in single layer in large Dutch oven. Drizzle oil over. Tuck potatoes between chicken pieces. Sprinkle with garlic and turmeric. Season with salt and pepper. Lay lemon slices over. Sprinkle with raisins. Pour over enough broth barely to cover chicken. Bring to boil over high heat. Cover and boil 10 minutes. Uncover; reduce heat to medium and simmer until chicken is just cooked through and potatoes are tender, about 30 minutes. Transfer chicken and potatoes to platter. Tent with foil to keep warm. Add lemon juice to Dutch oven. Boil cooking liquid until thickened to light sauce consistency and reduce by half, about 7 minutes. Season to taste with salt and pepper. Spoon over chicken and serve.

CHICKEN TIKKA KEBABS
6 SERVINGS

2 pounds skinless boneless chicken
  breast halves, cut into 1-inch
  pieces
¼ cup fresh lemon juice
½ teaspoon salt

¼ cup plain yogurt
4 garlic cloves, minced
1½ tablespoons ground coriander
2 teaspoons ground cumin
1 teaspoon ground turmeric
⅛ teaspoon ground ginger
  Pinch of dried crushed red pepper

12 6- to 8-inch bamboo skewers,
  soaked in water 30 minutes
2 tablespoons (¼ stick) butter,
  melted
  Salt

Combine chicken, ¼ cup lemon juice and ½ teaspoon salt in medium bowl; let stand 30 minutes.

Mix ¼ cup plain yogurt, minced garlic, 1½ tablespoons coriander, 2 teaspoons cumin, 1 teaspoon turmeric, ⅛ teaspoon ginger and crushed red pepper in small bowl. Add to chicken and stir until chicken is well coated with spice mixture. Refrigerate chicken at least 3 hours or overnight.

Prepare barbecue (medium-high heat). Thread chicken on skewers, dividing equally. Brush chicken with melted butter. Season with salt. Grill kebabs until just cooked through, turning frequently, about 7 minutes.

SIAMESE CHICKEN CURRY

Accompany the curry with rice, broccoli and a variety of condiments like peanuts, chopped green onions, chutney, raisins and chopped bell pepper.

4 SERVINGS

3 tablespoons curry powder
2 tablespoons cider vinegar
3 tablespoons butter
1 onion, chopped
2 garlic cloves, chopped
2 tablespoons (generous) chopped fresh basil or 2 teaspoons dried
½ teaspoon dried crushed red pepper
1½ cups canned low-salt chicken broth
¾ cup whipping cream
¾ teaspoon coconut extract
2½ cups ½-inch pieces cooked chicken
Salt and pepper

Stir curry powder and vinegar in small bowl to blend. Melt butter in heavy large skillet over medium heat. Add onion and garlic; sauté until onion is translucent, about 6 minutes. Add curry mixture; stir 2 minutes. Add basil and crushed red pepper; stir 1 minute. Add broth, cream and coconut extract; boil until reduced to sauce consistency, about 6 minutes. Add chicken; stir until heated through. Season with salt and pepper.

SPICE IT UP

If you love preparing Indian food but have difficulty finding all the fixings, the Indian Spice Kitchen kit can help. It includes a collection of over 20 ingredients that are typically used in Indian cuisine, plus a recipe booklet by noted cookbook author Madhur Jaffrey.

CHICKEN CACCIATORE

4 SERVINGS

1 3½-pound chicken, cut into 6 pieces
Salt and pepper
½ cup all-purpose flour

6 tablespoons olive oil
¾ pound mushrooms, halved
2 green bell peppers, diced
1 onion, chopped
4 garlic cloves, chopped
1 teaspoon (generous) dried oregano
1 cup purchased marinara sauce
⅔ cup canned low-salt chicken broth
½ cup dry Marsala
3 tablespoons drained capers

Grated Parmesan cheese (optional)

Season chicken with salt and pepper. Place flour in plastic bag. Add chicken pieces and toss to coat completely.

Heat 3 tablespoons olive oil in heavy large skillet over medium-high heat. Add chicken pieces to skillet and sauté until brown, about 4 minutes per side. Transfer chicken to plate. Pour fat from skillet. Add remaining 3 tablespoons olive oil to skillet. Add halved mushrooms, diced green bell peppers, chopped onion, chopped garlic and oregano and sauté until onion is tender, about 10 minutes. Mix in marinara sauce, chicken broth, Marsala and capers. Return chicken pieces to skillet, spooning sauce over. Bring sauce to boil. Reduce heat to medium-low. Cover skillet and simmer until chicken is tender, about 20 minutes.

Using tongs, transfer chicken to large platter. Boil sauce until slightly thickened, about 5 minutes; spoon off fat. Spoon sauce over chicken. Serve, passing Parmesan separately, if desired.

Beef

BEEF AND BROCCOLI STIR-FRY

4 SERVINGS

¼ cup soy sauce
¼ cup dry sherry
1 tablespoon honey
1 tablespoon (packed) chopped garlic
2 teaspoons grated orange peel
1 pound flank steak, cut diagonally across grain into thin strips

1 large head broccoli, cut into florets

2 tablespoons vegetable oil
1 tablespoon cornstarch
Salt and pepper
Cooked white rice

Whisk first 5 ingredients in large bowl. Add meat; toss to coat. Cover and refrigerate at least 1 hour and up to 4 hours.

Blanch broccoli in large pot of boiling salted water 2 minutes. Drain. Rinse under cold water; drain well.

Heat oil in heavy large wok or skillet over high heat. Drain meat well, reserving marinade. Add cornstarch to reserved marinade and mix until smooth; set aside. Add meat to wok and stir-fry until almost cooked through, about 2 minutes. Add broccoli and stir-fry until crisp-tender, about 2 minutes. Add reserved marinade mixture and boil until sauce thickens and coats meat and broccoli, stirring constantly, about 2 minutes. Season to taste with salt and pepper. Serve over rice.

Beef Bourguignon

8 SERVINGS

8 ounces bacon, coarsely chopped
3 pounds well-trimmed boneless
   beef chuck, cut into 1½-inch
   cubes (from 7-bone chuck roast)
   Salt and pepper
⅓ cup all-purpose flour
1¼ pounds boiling onions, peeled
¾ pound large carrots, cut into
   1-inch pieces
12 large garlic cloves, peeled
   (left whole)

3 cups canned beef broth
½ cup Cognac or brandy
2 750-ml bottles red Burgundy wine
1¼ pounds mushrooms
⅓ cup chopped fresh thyme or
   2 tablespoons dried
1 tablespoon dark brown sugar
1 tablespoon tomato paste

Preheat oven to 325°F. Sauté bacon in heavy large Dutch oven over high heat until brown and crisp, about 8 minutes. Using slotted spoon, transfer bacon to paper towels. Season beef generously with salt and pepper; coat with ⅓ cup flour, using all of flour. Working in 3 batches, brown beef in same pot over high heat, about 5 minutes per batch. Transfer meat to large bowl. Add onions and carrots to same pot and sauté until light brown, about 6 minutes. Add garlic and sauté 1 minute. Transfer vegetables to bowl with beef.

Add 1 cup broth and Cognac to pot; boil until reduced to glaze, scraping up browned bits, about 8 minutes. Return meat and vegetables and their juices to pot. Add wine, mushrooms, thyme, sugar, tomato paste and 2 cups broth. Bring to boil, stirring occasionally. Cover pot and place in oven. Cook until beef is tender, about 1 hour 20 minutes.

Ladle liquid from stew into large saucepan. Spoon off fat. Boil liquid until reduced to 2¾ cups, about 40 minutes. Season with salt and pepper. Pour liquid back over beef and vegetables. (*Can be prepared 1 day ahead.* Cover and chill.) Rewarm over low heat before serving.

Barbecued Flank Steak

This entreé is even better—and easier—if you place the meat in the marinade a day in advance.

4 SERVINGS

¼ cup soy sauce
¼ cup Worcestershire sauce
2 tablespoons fresh lemon juice
2 tablespoons chopped fresh
   cilantro
1 tablespoon minced fresh ginger
1 1¼-pound flank steak, fat trimmed

Whisk first 5 ingredients to blend in 13x9x2-inch glass baking dish. Add steak and turn to coat. Let stand 1 hour at room temperature or cover and refrigerate overnight, turning occasionally.

Prepare barbecue (medium-high heat) or preheat broiler. Drain marinade into small saucepan and bring to boil. Grill or broil steak about 5 minutes per side for rare. Transfer steak to platter; let stand 10 minutes. Thinly slice steak across grain. Pass marinade as sauce.

SOY SAUCE ENLIGHTENMENT

The condiment known as light soy sauce is not to be confused with some low-sodium soy sauces that also have the world "light" or "lite" on the label. Chinese cooks use both light soy sauce (sometimes colored with caramel), and a dark kind, which is aged longer and mixed with molasses for a deep, rich color and stronger flavor.

Light soy sauce is widely available in the United States, but if you have trouble finding it, you can order some from Rafal Spice Company. For more information, contact Rafal Spice Company, 2521 Russell Street, Detroit, MI 48207; 800-228-4276 or 313-259-6373.

SPICED BEEF WITH CHILIES AND VEGETABLES

4 SERVINGS

1 tablespoon olive oil
1 pound ground beef
1 small onion, chopped
4 garlic cloves, minced
1 14½-ounce can diced peeled tomatoes
12 ounces potatoes, peeled, diced
1 cup canned beef broth
1 large carrot, diced
2 serrano chilies or small jalapeño chilies, minced
2 teaspoons dried oregano
2 teaspoons chili powder
1 teaspoon ground cumin
½ teaspoon ground allspice

Heat oil in heavy large skillet over medium heat. Add beef, onion and garlic and sauté until beef is cooked through, breaking up beef with back of spoon, about 10 minutes. Add remaining ingredients and bring to boil. Reduce heat, cover and simmer until vegetables are tender, about 15 minutes. Uncover, increase heat and cook until liquid thickens slightly, about 5 minutes.

MARINATED FLANK STEAK

6 SERVINGS

4 large shallots, chopped
2 tablespoons olive oil
2 tablespoons fresh lemon juice
2 tablespoons dry red wine
1½ teaspoons dried thyme
Pepper
1 1½-pound flank steak, trimmed

Whisk first 5 ingredients to blend in 13x9x2-inch glass dish; season with pepper. Add steak and turn to coat. Marinate steak up to 2 hours at room temperature or cover and refrigerate up to 1 day, turning steak occasionally.

Preheat broiler. Remove steak from marinade. Broil steak to desired doneness, about 5 minutes per side for medium-rare. Transfer steak to platter.

Veal

VEAL CHOPS WITH DOUBLE-MUSTARD SAUCE

4 SERVINGS

8 tablespoons (1 stick) butter,
　room temperature
3 tablespoons minced shallots
2 tablespoons Dijon mustard
1½ tablespoons chopped fresh
　tarragon
1 tablespoon coarse-grained
　French mustard
　Pepper

4 veal chops (about ½ to
　¾ inch thick)
2 teaspoons Dijon mustard
4 teaspoons whole mustard seeds
　Salt and pepper
⅔ cup dry vermouth

Combine 7 tablespoons butter with next
4 ingredients in bowl. Season mustard

butter with pepper. *(Can be made 4 days ahead. Cover and refrigerate.)*

Brush veal with 2 teaspoons Dijon mustard. Press 1 teaspoon mustard seeds onto 1 side of each veal chop. Season with salt and pepper. Melt remaining 1 tablespoon butter in heavy large skillet over medium heat. Add veal and cook until just cooked through, about 4 minutes per side. Transfer to plate; cover with foil and keep warm. Add vermouth to drippings in skillet; boil until liquid is reduced to ¼ cup, about 3 minutes. Whisk in mustard butter. Season to taste with salt and pepper. Drizzle sauce over veal and serve.

BRAISED VEAL SHANKS WITH PORCINI AND POTATOES

4 SERVINGS

1 ounce dried porcini mushrooms
2 cups hot water

4 tablespoons olive oil
2 large onions, chopped
2 garlic cloves, chopped
2 teaspoons dried rosemary
2 bay leaves
1 pound button mushrooms, sliced
3 large red-skinned potatoes,
　cut into ½-inch-thick slices

6 1-inch-thick veal shanks
　Salt and pepper
　All-purpose flour
1 cup dry white wine
1½ cups canned beef broth
2 tablespoons fresh lemon juice

1 10-ounce package frozen peas,
　thawed

3 tablespoons chopped fresh parsley
1 tablespoon chopped lemon peel

Place porcini in bowl. Pour water over; let stand until soft, about 30 minutes. Drain, reserving liquid. Chop porcini.

Preheat oven to 350°F. Heat 2 tablespoons oil in heavy large Dutch oven over medium-high heat. Add onions, garlic, rosemary and bay leaves; sauté until tender, about 10 minutes. Add fresh and dried mushrooms and potatoes; cook 4 minutes, stirring occasionally.

Heat 2 tablespoons oil in heavy large skillet over high heat. Season veal with salt and pepper. Coat with flour. Add to skillet; brown well, about 4 minutes per side. Place atop vegetables in Dutch oven. Add wine to skillet; bring to boil, stirring up any browned bits. Boil until liquid is reduced by half, about 3 minutes. Add to Dutch oven. Add porcini soaking liquid, leaving any sediment behind. Add broth and juice. Bring to boil. Cover, place in oven and bake until veal is tender, about 1 hour 15 minutes. *(Can be made 1 day ahead. Cover; chill.)*

Uncover stew; cook over medium-high heat until liquid is thickened, stirring occasionally, about 15 minutes. Season with salt and pepper. Discard bay leaves. Add peas; cook until heated through.

Mix parsley and lemon peel in bowl. Top stew with parsley mixture and serve.

THE MUSTARD OF DIJON

Dijon mustard, regulated by French law with an *appellation d'origine contrôlée* similar to that for wine, can be manufactured anywhere in France as long as the mustard meets certain standards. It must always be smooth, pale yellow, creamy and pungent.

What best defines Dijon-style mustard, however, are those hardy little seeds. Even though they no longer must come from Dijon (today, in fact, many are imported from North America), they must be the spicier black, brown or yellow seeds of the mustard plant.

The ground seeds may be mixed with verjuice (the fermented juice of unripened grapes), white wine vinegar or wine, in addition to water, salt and spices. No food coloring or nonorganic chemical preservatives are permitted.

Mustard's tangy bite comes from an enzyme that is released when the ground seed is combined with liquid. According to French chef and cooking instructor Jacques Pépin, when you open a jar of Dijon mustard, it should be so sharp "it should make you cry, like horseradish."

Pork

U.S.A.

SMOTHERED PORK CHOPS WITH BLUE CHEESE-APPLEJACK GRAVY

4 SERVINGS

8 bacon slices, chopped
2 large onions, thinly sliced
2 large Granny Smith apples, peeled, cored, each cut into 8 wedges
1 tablespoon sugar

2 tablespoons all-purpose flour
1 cup apple juice
1 cup canned chicken broth
½ cup applejack or other apple brandy
1 cup crumbled Maytag blue cheese
Salt and pepper

4 6-ounce pork loin chops (about ¾ inch thick)

Cook bacon in heavy large skillet over medium heat until crisp. Transfer to paper towels. Spoon off 1 tablespoon drippings from skillet and reserve; discard all but 2 tablespoons remaining drippings in skillet. Add onions to skillet and sauté until golden, about 15 minutes. Push onions to 1 side of skillet; add apples and sugar to skillet and sauté until apples are golden, about 20 minutes. Transfer mixture to bowl.

Heat 1 tablespoon reserved bacon drippings in same skillet. Add flour and stir 1 minute. Gradually whisk in juice, broth and applejack. Boil until gravy thickens, whisking frequently, about 4 minutes. Add cheese and whisk until melted. Season with salt and pepper. Add onion mixture to gravy and stir until heated through. Remove from heat. Cover and keep warm.

Season pork with salt and pepper. Heat large nonstick skillet over medium heat. Add pork and sauté until cooked through, about 6 minutes per side. Transfer to bowl. Pour gravy over. Top with bacon and serve.

ROAST PORK WITH CABBAGE AND CARAWAY

6 SERVINGS

4 teaspoons caraway seeds, crushed in mortar with pestle
2 large garlic cloves, minced
2 teaspoons salt
1 teaspoon ground pepper
1 3-pound boneless double-loin center-cut pork roast*

3 tablespoons olive oil
1 large onion, sliced
4 carrots, peeled, sliced on diagonal
2 bay leaves
1 2½-pound head green cabbage, quartered, cored, sliced

1 12-ounce can beer
2 tablespoons light unsulfured molasses
1 cup canned beef broth

Combine 2 teaspoons caraway, garlic,

salt and pepper in bowl. Place pork in glass baking dish. Rub pork with spice mixture. Cover and chill up to 24 hours.

Preheat oven to 350°F. Heat 1 tablespoon oil in large skillet over medium-high heat. Add onion, carrots, bay leaves and 1 teaspoon caraway; sauté until softened, about 8 minutes. Transfer to roasting pan. Heat ½ tablespoon oil in same skillet over high heat. Add half of cabbage and ½ teaspoon caraway; sauté until cabbage begins to wilt, about 4 minutes. Repeat with ½ tablespoon oil, half of cabbage and ½ teaspoon caraway. Add to onion mixture; mix to blend. Season with salt and pepper.

Heat 1 tablespoon oil in same skillet over high heat. Add pork; brown on all sides, about 10 minutes. Set atop vegetables in pan. Add beer and molasses to skillet; bring to boil, scraping up browned bits. Pour over vegetables. Add broth.

Roast pork and vegetables 45 minutes. Turn pork over and roast until thermometer inserted into thick part registers 150°F; about 45 minutes. Place pork on work surface. Discard bay leaves. Using slotted spoon, place vegetables on platter. Slice pork; place atop vegetables. Transfer cooking juices to small saucepan. Boil 5 minutes. Spoon over pork.

This is made by tying two boneless pork loins together. If you can't find one, ask your butcher to prepare it for you.

Lamb

CHINA

MINCED LAMB WITH GINGER, HOISIN AND GREEN ONIONS

Serve this quick stir-fry with rice.

4 SERVINGS

2 tablespoons orange juice
1 tablespoon cornstarch
1 pound ground lamb
1 tablespoon Oriental sesame oil
2 tablespoons minced peeled fresh
  ginger
1 tablespoon minced fresh garlic
1 tablespoon minced orange peel
1 bunch green onions, chopped
¼ cup hoisin sauce*
  Butter lettuce leaves

Combine orange juice and cornstarch in small bowl. Sauté lamb in heavy large skillet over high heat until cooked through, breaking up with back of spoon, about 5 minutes. Pour lamb with its juices into colander; drain. Heat oil in same skillet over high heat. Add ginger, garlic and orange peel; stir-fry 30 seconds. Add green onions and stir-fry 1 minute. Add hoisin sauce and lamb to skillet; stir until blended. Add orange juice mixture; stir until thickened, about 1 minute. Spoon into lettuce leaves.

Available at Asian markets and in the Asian section of some supermarkets.

MEDITERRANEAN

MEDITERRANEAN VEGETABLE AND LAMB STEW

6 SERVINGS

2 tablespoons olive oil
2½ pounds lamb shoulder-blade roast or lamb shoulder-blade chops, trimmed, meat cut into ¾-inch pieces, bones reserved
  Salt and pepper
2 large onions, chopped
2½ teaspoons ground cumin
1 teaspoon ground cinnamon
1 28-ounce can crushed tomatoes with added puree
1 14½-ounce can chicken broth
1 14½-ounce can beef broth
2 bay leaves

3 Japanese eggplants, halved lengthwise, cut crosswise into ¾-inch pieces
2 large red bell peppers, seeded, cut into ¾-inch cubes
3 large white-skinned potatoes,

cut into 1-inch pieces
1 1½-pound butternut squash, peeled, seeded, cut into 1-inch pieces
2 15- to 16-ounce cans garbanzo beans (chickpeas), rinsed, drained
3 zucchini, halved lengthwise, cut crosswise into ½-inch pieces
3 tablespoons chopped fresh marjoram or 1 tablespoon dried
2 tablespoons honey
½ teaspoon cayenne pepper

Heat oil in heavy large Dutch oven over medium-high heat. Season lamb meat with salt and pepper. Working in batches, add lamb meat and bones to pot and brown on all sides. Using slotted spoon, transfer lamb and bones to plate. Add onions to Dutch oven and sauté until tender and brown, about 10 minutes. Add cumin and cinnamon and stir until aromatic, about 30 seconds. Add tomatoes, chicken broth, beef broth and bay leaves. Return lamb, bones and any accumulated juices to Dutch oven. Bring to boil. Reduce heat,

cover and simmer 30 minutes.

Add eggplants, bell peppers, potatoes, butternut squash and beans and bring to simmer. Cover and cook until lamb and vegetables are tender, stirring occasionally, about 45 minutes. Uncover and simmer until liquid thickens, about 20 minutes. Discard lamb bones and bay leaves. (*Can be made 1 day ahead. Cool slightly. Cover and refrigerate. Bring to simmer before continuing.*) Add zucchini and marjoram to stew and simmer until zucchini is tender, about 5 minutes. Stir in honey and cayenne. Season with salt and pepper and serve.

Vegetarian

MEXICO

CHEESE ENCHILADAS WITH GREEN SAUCE

6 SERVINGS

SAUCE
½ 10-ounce package frozen chopped spinach

1 tablespoon butter
1 tablespoon all-purpose flour
1 cup whipping cream
1 cup milk
6 tablespoons chopped fresh cilantro
3 green onions, minced
½ 4-ounce can diced green chilies, drained
1¾ teaspoons ground cumin
1½ teaspoons ground coriander
¼ teaspoon dried crushed red pepper
Salt and pepper

ENCHILADAS
½ cup vegetable oil
12 6-inch corn tortillas
3 cups grated mild cheddar cheese
1½ cups grated Monterey Jack cheese
½ cup finely chopped onion
1 tablespoon chopped fresh cilantro

½ cup sour cream

FOR SAUCE: Cook spinach according to package instructions. Drain well. Set aside. Melt butter in heavy medium skillet over medium heat. Add flour and stir mixture 2 minutes; do not brown. Gradually whisk in whipping cream and milk. Simmer until thickened, about 5 minutes. Stir in spinach, cilantro, green onions, chilies, cumin, coriander and red pepper. Puree in batches in processor until almost smooth. Season with salt and pepper. *(Can be prepared 1 day ahead. Cover and refrigerate. Bring to room temperature before using.)*

FOR ENCHILADAS: Heat oil in heavy small skillet over medium-high heat. Using tongs, briefly dip each tortilla in oil to soften, about 15 seconds per side. Transfer to paper towels and drain. Combine cheeses in large bowl; set aside 1½ cups for topping. Combine onion and cilantro in small bowl. Place ¼ cup cheese mixture in center of 1 tortilla. Spoon 2 teaspoons onion mixture over. Roll up tortilla. Place seam side down in large glass baking dish. Repeat with remaining tortillas, cheese and onion, using ¼ cup cheese for each. *(Can be made 1 day ahead. Cover and chill.)*

Preheat oven to 375°F. Stir sour cream into sauce; pour over enchiladas. Sprinkle with reserved 1½ cups cheese. Bake until cheese melts and enchiladas are heated through, about 25 minutes.

VEGETABLE COUSCOUS WITH FETA CHEESE
8 SERVINGS

2 tablespoons olive oil
½ cup chopped red onion
3 garlic cloves, minced
4 red-skinned potatoes,
  cut into ½-inch pieces
3 carrots, cut diagonally into
  ½-inch-thick slices
2 small zucchini, cut into
  ½-inch-thick slices
1 tablespoon chili powder
1 teaspoon paprika
1 teaspoon curry powder
½ teaspoon ground cumin
½ teaspoon turmeric
  Generous pinch of ground
  cinnamon

1 15-ounce can tomato sauce
½ cup water
  Salt and pepper

1 10-ounce box couscous
1 cup crumbled feta cheese
  (about 4 ounces)

Heat oil in heavy large skillet over medium-high heat. Add onion and garlic and sauté until tender, about 4 minutes. Add potatoes and carrots and sauté 5 minutes. Add zucchini, chili powder, paprika, curry powder, cumin, turmeric and cinnamon and stir until spices are fragrant, about 1 minute. Add tomato sauce and ½ cup water. Bring to boil. Reduce heat, cover and simmer 10 minutes. Uncover and simmer until potatoes are tender and sauce is slightly thickened, about 10 minutes. Season to taste with salt and pepper. *(Can be prepared 1 day ahead. Cover and refrigerate.)*

Cook couscous according to package directions. Transfer couscous to large bowl. Bring vegetable mixture to simmer. Pour over couscous. Sprinkle with feta cheese and serve.

Pastas, Risottos, Pizzas & Sandwiches

Enlightened eaters everywhere are turning to main courses featuring pasta, grains and breads, aware that they offer a maximum of healthful carbohydrates and a minimum of fat. The recipes that follow prove that cooks worldwide have long known the wisdom of these ways. From Mexican Fideo to Asian Noodles with Ginger-Cilantro Sauce, Italian Roasted Garlic and Wild Mushroom Risotto to Scandinavian Open-Face Bay Shrimp Sandwiches, this chapter abounds with healthful satisfaction.

Pastas

ITALY

PASTA WITH RICOTTA AND FRESH HERBS

4 SERVINGS

1 15-ounce container low-fat
ricotta cheese
⅔ cup nonfat milk
½ cup grated Parmesan cheese
2 teaspoons olive oil
1 cup chopped onion
2 garlic cloves, chopped
½ cup chopped fresh basil
¼ cup chopped fresh chives
or green onions
¼ cup chopped fresh parsley
12 ounces rotelle or fusilli pasta,
freshly cooked
Salt and pepper

Blend ricotta cheese, milk and Parmesan in processor until smooth. Heat oil in heavy large skillet over medium heat. Add onion; sauté until beginning to brown, about 5 minutes. Add garlic and sauté 2 minutes. Add ricotta mixture, basil, chives and parsley to skillet; stir until heated through, about 5 minutes. Mix in rotelle. Season with salt and pepper.

MEXICO

SAUTÉED PASTA WITH TOMATOES AND GARLIC (FIDEO)

2 SERVINGS

3 tablespoons olive oil
8 ounces coil fideo or angel hair
pasta, broken in half
1 14½-ounce can diced peeled
tomatoes
1 cup tomato juice
1 cup water
4 large garlic cloves, chopped
1 teaspoon dried oregano
Chopped fresh parsley

Heat oil in heavy large skillet over high heat. Add fideo and sauté until brown, about 3 minutes. Add tomatoes with their liquids, tomato juice, water, garlic and oregano. Cover and simmer until fideo is tender, stirring occasionally, about 16 minutes. Transfer to bowl. Garnish with parsley and serve.

CHINA

ASIAN NOODLES WITH GINGER-CILANTRO SAUCE

4 SERVINGS

1 12-ounce package fresh Oriental-
style water noodles or linguine
3 tablespoons Oriental sesame oil

2 tablespoons minced peeled fresh
ginger
1 small jalapeño chili, seeded
1 cup (packed) fresh cilantro leaves
1 tablespoon soy sauce
1 tablespoon rice vinegar
1 tablespoon creamy peanut butter
3 tablespoons (or more) canned
chicken broth
Salt and pepper

Cook noodles in large pot of boiling salted water until just tender but still firm to bite. Drain noodles. Rinse with cold water; drain well. Transfer to large bowl. Toss with 1 tablespoon sesame oil.

With processor running, drop ginger and chili through feed tube and mince. Add cilantro, soy sauce, vinegar, peanut butter, 3 tablespoons broth and remaining 2 tablespoons sesame oil. Process until mixture is almost smooth, adding more broth if necessary. Season to taste with salt and pepper. Add sauce to noodles and toss.

ITALY

LINGUINE WITH WHITE CLAM SAUCE

4 SERVINGS

2 tablespoons olive oil
½ cup chopped fresh parsley (preferably Italian)
8 garlic cloves, chopped
4 6½-ounce cans chopped clams, drained, juices reserved
½ cup whipping cream
¼ cup dry white wine
1 tablespoon white wine Worcestershire sauce
½ teaspoon garlic salt

¼ teaspoon ground white pepper
¼ teaspoon cayenne pepper
1 pound linguine, freshly cooked
Salt and pepper
Grated Parmesan cheese (optional)

Heat olive oil in heavy large Dutch oven over medium-high heat. Add chopped parsley and chopped garlic and sauté until garlic just begins to color, about 45 seconds. Add reserved clam juices, whipping cream, dry white wine, Worcestershire sauce, garlic salt, white pepper and cayenne pepper. Simmer until mixture is reduced to thin sauce consistency, about 10 minutes. Add chopped clams and freshly cooked linguine to pot and toss until sauce coats pasta thickly, about 5 minutes. Season to taste with salt and pepper. Serve, passing Parmesan, if desired.

ITALY

(Cover Recipe)

PASTA WITH SHRIMP AND BASIL VINAIGRETTE

4 SERVINGS

5 tablespoons fresh lemon juice

2 tablespoons Dijon mustard
⅓ cup plus 2 tablespoons olive oil
2 ½-ounce packages fresh basil leaves, chopped (about ¾ cup)
1½ pounds uncooked medium shrimp, peeled, deveined
Salt and pepper

1 pound gnocchi pasta or orecchiette pasta

4 zucchini, halved lengthwise
Olive oil
Freshly grated Parmesan cheese (optional)

Prepare barbecue (medium-high heat) or preheat broiler. Combine 4 tablespoons fresh lemon juice and Dijon mustard in small bowl. Gradually mix in ⅓ cup olive oil. Mix in chopped fresh basil. Place shrimp in medium bowl. Drizzle with remaining 1 tablespoon fresh lemon juice and 2 tablespoons olive oil. Toss to coat. Season with salt and pepper.

Cook pasta in large pot of boiling salted water until just tender but still firm to bite, stirring occasionally.

Meanwhile, brush zucchini on both sides with oil. Season with salt and pepper. Grill until charred, about 2 minutes per side. Transfer to plate. Add shrimp to grill and cook until just cooked through, about 2 minutes per side. Transfer to large bowl. Cut zucchini crosswise into 1-inch pieces and add to shrimp.

Drain pasta well. Add to bowl with shrimp and zucchini. Add basil vinaigrette and toss to coat. Season to taste with salt and pepper. (*Can be prepared up to 1 hour ahead. Let stand at room temperature.*) Serve pasta warm or at room temperature, passing grated Parmesan cheese, if desired.

ITALY

Roasted Garlic and Wild Mushroom Risotto

6 SERVINGS

2 large heads garlic (about 40 cloves), cloves separated, unpeeled
4 tablespoons olive oil
¾ ounce dried porcini mushrooms*

¾ pound mixed fresh wild mushrooms (such as shiitake and crimini, stems trimmed from shiitake), sliced
Salt and pepper

1 cup chopped shallots
2 tablespoons chopped fresh thyme or 2 teaspoons dried
1½ cups arborio rice* or medium-grain white rice
½ cup dry white wine
3½ to 4 cups canned low-salt chicken broth
2 cups thinly sliced fresh spinach leaves
⅓ cup freshly grated Parmesan cheese (about 1 ounce)

Preheat oven to 400°F. Combine garlic and 2 tablespoons oil in small baking dish. Bake until garlic is golden and tender when pierced with small sharp knife, stirring occasionally, about 50 minutes. Cool slightly; peel garlic. Chop enough garlic to measure ¼ cup packed (*refrigerate remaining garlic for another use*).

Place porcini in small bowl. Pour enough hot water over to cover. Let stand until soft, about 30 minutes. Drain porcini. Squeeze porcini dry and coarsely chop.

Heat 1 tablespoon oil in large non-stick skillet over medium-high heat. Add fresh mushrooms and sauté until golden and juices evaporate, about 7 minutes. Add porcini and stir 1 minute. Season with salt and pepper. Set aside.

Heat 1 tablespoon oil in heavy medium saucepan over medium-high heat. Add shallots and thyme and sauté until tender, about 4 minutes. Add rice and stir to coat with shallot mixture. Add wine and cook until almost evaporated. Mix in chopped garlic and 3½ cups chicken broth and bring to boil. Reduce heat to medium and cook until rice is tender and mixture is creamy, stirring occasionally and adding more broth if risotto is dry, about 20 minutes. Add mushroom mixture and spinach. Stir until spinach wilts. Stir in Parmesan cheese. Season to taste with salt and pepper.

Dried porcini mushrooms and arborio rice are available at Italian markets, specialty foods stores and some supermarkets.

Pizzas

SPINACH, GORGONZOLA AND PINE NUT PIZZA

MAKES 1 LARGE PIZZA

1 tablespoon olive oil
1 onion, sliced
2 garlic cloves, minced
1 10-ounce package frozen spinach leaves, thawed, drained well, squeezed dry

1 12-inch-diameter baked cheese pizza crust (such as Boboli)
1 tablespoon Garlic Oil (see recipe)
4 ounces Gorgonzola cheese, crumbled
3 ounces grated mozzarella cheese
¼ cup pine nuts (about 1 ounce)
Pepper

Heat oil in heavy large skillet over medium heat. Add onion and sauté until very tender and golden, about 10 minutes. Add garlic; sauté 2 minutes.

Add spinach to skillet and cook until liquid evaporates, separating spinach leaves with spoon, about 3 minutes. Cool. (*Can be prepared 1 day ahead. Cover and chill.*)

Preheat oven to 450°F. Place crust on baking sheet. Brush crust with Garlic Oil. Top with spinach mixture. Sprinkle Gorgonzola and mozzarella over spinach. Top with nuts. Season with pepper.

Bake pizza until crust is golden brown and cheese bubbles, about 15 minutes. Transfer to cutting board. Cool 5 minutes. Cut into wedges and serve.

GARLIC OIL

Here's an easy, flavorful oil for pizzas. Leftover oil is great for bruschetta—just brush it on crusty Italian bread slices, place them under the broiler until they're lightly toasted and top with chopped tomatoes and basil. Be sure to prepare the oil the day before using; store it in the refrigerator.

MAKES ¼ CUP

½ cup olive oil
6 large garlic cloves, pressed

Combine olive oil and garlic. Cover and chill overnight. (*Can be made 2 days ahead; keep chilled.*) Let stand at room temperature 30 minutes before using.

MAJORCAN "PIZZA"

Known as coca, this is the traditional street food of Palma. The name derives from the Latin verb coquere, *which means "to cook." Shaped in a long oval or rectangle, baked in a wood-fired oven and sold in room-temperature squares, coca is usually eaten as a snack, but it can also be a great starter for a casual meal. Unlike its Italian counterpart, it is covered only with vegetables, never with cheese. There are sweet cocas and special holiday versions, too. When made with frozen bread dough, coca is a snap to prepare.*

MAKES 2 COCAS (8 SERVINGS)

2 1-pound loaves frozen white bread dough, thawed, room temperature
9 tablespoons olive oil

½ teaspoon ground black pepper

2 medium onions, chopped
5 large garlic cloves, minced
2 large red bell peppers, chopped
1 large bunch green Swiss chard,
    ribs removed and thinly sliced,
    leaves thinly sliced
Salt and pepper

Place each loaf of bread dough in separate bowl. Add 1 tablespoon oil to each; season each with ¼ teaspoon pepper. Knead each in bowl until oil is well incorporated, about 3 minutes. Let dough rest in bowls 10 minutes.

Oil two 15x10-inch baking sheets. Turn out dough onto floured surface; knead 1 minute. Roll out each dough piece to irregular 13x9-inch rectangle, pulling and stretching dough. Transfer each to prepared sheet. Brush each with 1 tablespoon oil. Let dough rise uncovered in warm draft-free area until puffy, about 30 minutes.

Meanwhile, preheat oven to 400°F. Heat 3 tablespoons oil in heavy large skillet over medium heat. Add onions and garlic; sauté 1 minute. Add bell peppers and chard ribs and sauté until tender, about 10 minutes. Add chard leaves and stir until just wilted and coated with oil, about 3 minutes. Season with salt and pepper.

Press dough all over with fingers, forming indentations. Brush each with 1 tablespoon oil. Spread vegetables over, leaving 1-inch border. Bake until crusts are golden, about 25 minutes. Serve at room temperature.

Seafood Pizza

This pizza manages to break a cardinal rule of Italian cooking: You're not supposed to mix cheese and fish, but in this case the partnership is a winner.

MAKES 1 LARGE PIZZA

12 mussels, scrubbed, debearded
½ cup dry white wine
14 sun-dried tomatoes (not packed
    in oil), chopped
 4 large garlic cloves, minced
 1 large shallot, minced

 1 cup canned crushed tomatoes
    with added puree
½ teaspoon grated lemon peel
¼ teaspoon dried crushed red pepper

10 large uncooked shrimp, peeled,
    deveined, cut in half lengthwise
 5 ounces bay scallops
Salt and pepper

 1 12-inch-diameter baked cheese
    pizza crust (such as Boboli)

1 tablespoon Garlic Oil (see recipe)
¾ cup grated mozzarella cheese
   (about 3 ounces)
1 tablespoon minced fresh basil or
   1 teaspoon dried
2 tablespoons freshly grated
   Parmesan cheese

Combine first 5 ingredients in heavy large skillet over medium-high heat. Cover; boil just until mussels open, shaking pan occasionally, about 4 minutes. Using tongs, transfer mussels to work surface, discarding any that do not open.

Add crushed tomatoes, lemon peel and dried red pepper to same skillet. Stir over medium-high heat until sauce is thick, about 4 minutes. Remove mussels from shells; discard shells and place mussels in small bowl. (*Mussels and sauce can be prepared 1 day ahead. Cover separately and refrigerate.*)

Preheat oven to 450°F. Bring sauce to simmer over medium-high heat. Add shrimp and scallops and cook until seafood is almost cooked through, about 3 minutes. Remove from heat.

Cool 10 minutes. Stir in mussels. Season to taste with salt and pepper.

Place crust on large baking sheet. Brush with Garlic Oil. Bake crust until golden brown and edges begin to crisp, about 10 minutes. Stir mozzarella and basil into seafood mixture. Spoon over hot crust. Sprinkle with Parmesan.

Bake pizza until shrimp and scallops are cooked through and mozzarella cheese melts, about 6 minutes. Transfer pizza to cutting board. Cool 5 minutes. Cut into wedges and serve.

ITALY

Artichoke Pizza with Goat Cheese and Sausage

For a good meatless main course, simply omit the Italian sausage.

MAKES 1 LARGE PIZZA

1 pound sweet Italian sausage,
   casings removed

1 13.75- to 14-ounce can artichoke
   hearts, drained
⅓ cup roasted red bell peppers from
   jar, drained
20 Kalamata olives,* pitted
2 tablespoons chopped fresh basil
   or 2 teaspoons dried
1 cup grated mozzarella cheese
   (about 4 ounces)
⅓ cup freshly grated Parmesan
   cheese (about 1 ounce)

1 12-inch-diameter baked cheese
   pizza crust (such as Boboli)
1 tablespoon Garlic Oil (see recipe)
½ cup (generous) crumbled soft
   fresh goat cheese (such as
   Montrachet; about 2 ounces)
   Pepper

Sauté sausage in heavy medium skillet over medium heat until cooked through, crumbling sausage with spoon, about 10 minutes. Using slotted spoon, transfer all sausage to paper towels and drain.

Combine artichoke hearts, bell peppers, 12 olives and basil in processor. Using on/off turns, process until finely chopped. Transfer mixture to large bowl. Stir in sausage and mozzarella and

Parmesan cheeses. *(Can be prepared 1 day ahead. Cover and refrigerate.)*

Preheat oven to 450°F. Place crust on large baking sheet. Brush with Garlic Oil. Spread artichoke mixture over crust. Dot with goat cheese. Top with 8 olives. Season with pepper. Bake pizza until crust is golden and mozzarella bubbles, about 15 minutes. Transfer to cutting board. Cool 5 minutes. Cut into wedges.

Black, brine-cured Kalamata olives are available at Greek and Italian markets and some supermarkets.

Sandwiches

SCANDINAVIAN OPEN-FACE BAY SHRIMP SANDWICH

4 SERVINGS

½ cup mayonnaise
½ cup chopped fresh dill
4 teaspoons Dijon mustard
2 teaspoons fresh lemon juice
 Salt and pepper
4 egg or pumpernickel bread slices, toasted
1 pound cooked bay shrimp, drained, patted dry
4 butter lettuce leaves
½ English hothouse cucumber, thinly sliced
4 tomato wedges
4 thin lemon slices
4 fresh dill sprigs

Combine first 4 ingredients in medium bowl. Season with salt and pepper. Spread 1 tablespoon dressing over each bread slice. Mix shrimp into remaining dressing. Place 1 lettuce leaf on each bread slice pressing to adhere. Arrange 6 cucumber slices atop lettuce on each slice. Arrange shrimp mixture atop cucumbers. Garnish each sandwich with tomato wedge, lemon slice and dill sprig.

GRILLED CHEDDAR CHEESE AND HAM SANDWICHES

4 SERVINGS

¼ cup (½ stick) butter, room temperature
1 tablespoon Dijon mustard
2 teaspoons minced fresh thyme
2 teaspoons minced fresh parsley
 Salt and pepper
8 6x4-inch slices country-style bread (about ½ inch thick)
½ pound cheddar cheese, thinly sliced
¼ pound thinly sliced smoked ham
½ small red onion, thinly sliced
1 large tomato, thinly sliced

Mix first 4 ingredients in bowl. Season with salt and pepper. Arrange 4 bread slices on work surface. Divide half of cheese equally among bread slices. Top with ham, then onion, tomato and remaining cheese. Top sandwiches with remaining bread. Spread herb butter on outside of sandwich tops and bottoms.

Heat large nonstick skillet over medium heat. Add sandwiches and cook until bottoms are golden, about 3 minutes. Turn sandwiches over, cover skillet and cook until cheese melts and bread is golden, about 3 minutes.

LAMB BURGERS IN PITA WITH YOGURT SAUCE

Called tzatziki *in Greece, this yogurt sauce can also be used on a baked potato as a nonfat alternative to sour cream. To prevent the pita bread in this recipe from getting soggy, place the trimmed portion of the bread down into the pocket to act as a sponge for the lamb drippings and yogurt.*

4 SERVINGS

2 cups plain nonfat yogurt
½ medium onion, chopped
½ cucumber, peeled, seeded, diced
1 tablespoon minced garlic
2 teaspoons fresh lemon juice
  Salt and pepper

1 pound ground lamb
⅔ cup fresh white breadcrumbs
½ medium onion, chopped
2 tablespoons chopped fresh parsley
4 teaspoons minced garlic
1¼ teaspoons dried oregano

4 pita bread rounds, top ¼ trimmed

from each (tops reserved)
4 lettuce leaves

Mix first 5 ingredients together in medium bowl. Season yogurt sauce to taste with salt and pepper.

Mix lamb and next 5 ingredients in large bowl until well blended. Season generously with salt and pepper. Shape mixture into four ¾-inch-thick patties.

Preheat broiler. Place lamb patties on broiler rack and broil until cooked through, about 4 minutes per side.

Open pita bread rounds; line bottoms with trimmed tops, if desired. Place lettuce, burger, then large spoonful of yogurt sauce in each round. Serve, passing extra sauce separately.

PAPRIKA PORK PATTIES

Serve these on toasted rye with grilled onions, roasted red peppers and sauerkraut.

6 SERVINGS

6 large garlic cloves
¼ pound bacon, diced

6 tablespoons ice water
4 teaspoons sweet Hungarian paprika
1 teaspoon hot Hungarian paprika
¾ teaspoon coarse salt
½ teaspoon black pepper
½ teaspoon ground allspice
1 pound ground pork
½ cup chopped drained sauerkraut

With processor running, drop garlic through feed tube and mince. Add next 7 ingredients and process until thick paste forms. Add pork and combine, using on/off turns. Add sauerkraut and just mix in. With moistened hands, shape sausage into six ¾-inch-thick patties; arrange on plate.

Heat large nonstick skillet over medium heat. Add sausage patties and cook until brown and just cooked through, about 6 minutes per side.

Breakfast & Brunch

The presence in this chapter of such recipes as Blueberry-Buckwheat Pancakes and Texas-Style Cinnamon French Toast bears out an impression that America reigns as the land of breakfast and brunch. Look closer, though, and you'll find specialties of other countries–from Mexican Scrambled Eggs to Tunisian *chakchouka*–to support the fact that people everywhere appreciate the value of starting the day with a good meal.

Pancakes & French Toast

JOHNNYCAKES WITH MAPLE SYRUP

These little cornmeal pancakes are served with butter and syrup. Assorted breakfast rolls and sliced melon round out the meal.

MAKES ABOUT 46

2 cups white cornmeal
2 teaspoons sugar
1½ teaspoons salt
3 cups boiling water

4 tablespoons (about) butter

Additional butter
Pure maple syrup

Preheat oven to 250°F. Mix cornmeal, sugar and salt in large bowl. Mix in 3 cups boiling water (batter will be thick). Melt 1 tablespoon butter on heavy large griddle or in large skillet over medium heat. Drop batter onto griddle by tablespoonfuls, spreading with back of spoon to 2-inch-diameter cakes. Cook until golden brown, about 4 minutes per side. Transfer to platter. Keep warm in oven. Repeat with remaining batter, adding more butter as needed.

Serve johnnycakes warm with additional butter and maple syrup.

BLUEBERRY-BUCKWHEAT PANCAKES

MAKES ABOUT 18

¾ cup unbleached all-purpose flour
½ cup buckwheat flour*
2 tablespoons sugar
1½ teaspoons baking powder
½ teaspoon salt
¼ teaspoon baking soda
2 cups buttermilk
2 tablespoons vegetable oil
2 large eggs, separated

Melted butter
1½ cups (about) fresh blueberries
   or frozen, unthawed

Mix first 6 ingredients in large bowl. Stir in buttermilk, oil and egg yolks. Using electric mixer, beat egg whites in medium bowl until medium-firm peaks form. Gently fold whites into batter.

Heat heavy large skillet over medium-high heat; lightly brush skillet with melted butter. Drop batter by ¼ cupfuls into skillet; spread to 4-inch rounds. Sprinkle 2 tablespoons blueberries over each round. Cook until tops are covered with small bubbles and bottoms are golden, about 2 minutes. Turn and cook until second sides are golden, about 1 minute. Repeat with remaining batter and blueberries, brushing skillet with melted butter for each batch.

Available at natural foods stores and some supermarkets.

HAM AND CHEESE GRIDDLE CAKES

4 SERVINGS

¾ cup yellow cornmeal
¾ cup unbleached all-purpose flour

1 teaspoon baking powder
¼ teaspoon baking soda
¼ teaspoon salt
1½ cups buttermilk
3 large eggs, separated
4 tablespoons (about) butter, melted
⅓ cup crumbled Maytag blue cheese
⅓ cup finely chopped ham

Maple syrup

Mix first 5 ingredients in large bowl to blend. Whisk buttermilk, egg yolks and 1½ tablespoons melted butter in medium bowl to blend. Whisk into dry ingredients. Mix in cheese and ham. Beat egg whites in another bowl to stiff peaks. Fold whites into batter in 2 additions.

Heat 1 tablespoon melted butter in large nonstick skillet over medium heat. Working in batches, pour batter into skillet by ¼ cupfuls. Cook until cakes are puffed and golden, adding more butter to skillet for each batch if necessary, about 3 minutes per side. Transfer to plates. Serve with maple syrup.

Texas-Style Cinnamon French Toast

The recipe yields two Texas-size portions or four servings for small appetites.

2 TO 4 SERVINGS

3 eggs
6 tablespoons half-and-half
1 tablespoon sugar
3 teaspoons ground cinnamon
¼ teaspoon vanilla extract
4 ¾-inch-thick slices soft-crusted
   French bread or egg bread

2 tablespoons (¼ stick) butter
¼ cup powdered sugar
   Warm maple syrup (optional)

Beat eggs, half-and-half, sugar, 2 teaspoons cinnamon and vanilla extract in 13x9x2-inch glass baking dish to blend. Add bread and turn to coat. Cover and chill until bread absorbs egg mixture, at least 30 minutes and up to 1 day.

Melt butter in heavy large skillet over medium heat. Add bread and cook until golden and cooked through, about 3 minutes per side. Transfer to plates. Combine powdered sugar with remaining 1 teaspoon cinnamon and sift over toast. Serve with maple syrup, if desired.

Eggs

Mexican Scrambled Eggs

6 SERVINGS

12 eggs
1 teaspoon salt
½ teaspoon pepper
¼ cup vegetable oil
4 5- to 6-inch corn tortillas,
   cut into 2x¼-inch strips
¼ cup chopped green onions
1 tablespoon minced seeded
   jalapeño chili
1 cup shredded Monterey Jack
   cheese
1 cup chopped seeded tomatoes
⅓ cup chopped fresh cilantro

Whisk eggs, salt and pepper in large bowl until well blended. Heat oil in 12-inch nonstick skillet over medium-high heat. Working in batches, add tortilla strips; cook just until softened, about 15 seconds per batch. Drain on paper towels. Add green onions and chili to skillet; stir 2 minutes. Reduce heat to medium. Add eggs and tortilla strips to skillet and stir until almost set, about 4 minutes. Add cheese, tomatoes and cilantro. Stir until eggs are set and cheese melts, about 1 minute. Serve immediately.

M E X I C O

TORTILLAS WITH EGGS

A twist on chilaquiles, a tortilla-based hash. It's great served with salsa for breakfast or brunch.

2 SERVINGS

1 tablespoon corn oil
3 5- to 6-inch corn tortillas, halved, cut crosswise into ½-inch-wide strips
4 eggs, beaten to blend

¼ cup canned diced green chilies
2 tablespoons chopped fresh cilantro
Hot pepper sauce (such as Tabasco)

Heat oil in heavy medium nonstick skillet over medium heat. Add tortillas and stir until softened, about 1 minute. Add eggs, chilies and cilantro. Stir until eggs softly set, about 3 minutes. Season with hot pepper sauce, salt and pepper.

PARTY FAVORITES

The cold-smoked trout and salmon from Tobermory Fish Farm in Scotland are a wonderful indulgence for New Year's brunches. Both the salmon and trout are available sliced or unsliced. Call 301-924-0595 to order.

T U N I S I A

SAUSAGE AND VEGETABLE SAUTÉ WITH EGGS

Called chakchouka, *this specialty is perfect for brunch, lunch or even a quick supper. Traditionally, it is prepared with a slender, spicy beef or lamb* merguez *sausage, and a soft bread is used in place of a fork to "grab and eat."*

6 SERVINGS

2 tablespoons olive oil
1 pound hot Italian sausages, cut into 1-inch lengths
2 medium-size red-skinned potatoes, unpeeled, cut into ½-inch pieces
2 medium onions, chopped
2 green bell peppers, chopped
1 jalapeño chili, chopped
4 medium tomatoes, seeded, chopped
½ cup water
6 eggs

Heat oil in heavy large skillet over

medium-high heat. Add sausages, potatoes, onions, bell peppers and chili and sauté until vegetables begin to soften, about 10 minutes. Add tomatoes and ½ cup water and bring to boil. Reduce heat to medium, cover skillet and simmer until vegetables are tender and sausage is cooked through, about 15 minutes. Uncover skillet; simmer until sauce is thick, about 8 minutes. One at a time, crack eggshells and drop eggs onto sausage mixture, spacing evenly. Cover and cook until egg whites are set and yolks still feel soft to touch, about 4 minutes. Serve immediately.

Hashes

U.S.A.

BLUE AND RED FLANNEL HASH

A great-tasting hash that gets its kick from the combination of Maytag blue cheese, spicy sausage, red bell pepper and beets.

4 SERVINGS

8 ounces hot Italian turkey
   sausages, casings removed
1 cup chopped red onion
3 tablespoons butter
¾ teaspoon dried thyme
1 10-ounce russet potato, peeled,
   cut into ½-inch cubes
1 cup chopped red bell pepper
   Salt and pepper

1 15-ounce can sliced pickled beets,
   drained, cut into ½-inch pieces
4 tablespoons chopped fresh parsley
¾ cup crumbled Maytag blue cheese

4 eggs

Heat large nonstick skillet over medium-high heat. Add sausage and sauté until cooked through, about 10 minutes. Using slotted spoon, transfer sausage to bowl. Add onion, 1 tablespoon butter and thyme to skillet; stir 3 minutes. Add potato and bell pepper; season with salt and pepper. Reduce heat to low. Cover and cook until potato is tender, stirring occasionally, about 10 minutes.

Increase heat to medium-high. Stir sausage, beets and half of parsley into potato. Cook without stirring until hash begins to brown on bottom, about 5 minutes. Using spatula, turn hash over by sections and cook without stirring until brown on bottom, about 5 minutes. Sprinkle cheese over. Remove from heat. Cover and let stand 5 minutes.

Melt 2 tablespoons butter in medium skillet over medium-high heat. Add eggs and fry to desired doneness.

Divide hash among plates; top with eggs. Sprinkle with remaining parsley.

SALMON HASH WITH HORSERADISH-DILL CREAM

This brunch dish makes delicious use of leftover cooked salmon or potatoes.

2 SERVINGS

1 12-ounce salmon fillet
  (about 1 inch thick)
  Salt and pepper
12 ounces small white potatoes

6 tablespoons chilled whipping
  cream
4 tablespoons prepared white
  horseradish
3 tablespoons chopped fresh dill
½ teaspoon white wine vinegar

½ cup chopped green onions
2 tablespoons unsalted butter

Preheat oven to 350°F. Place salmon on baking sheet; season with salt and pepper. Bake just until cooked through, about 18 minutes. Transfer to plate. Cover; chill until cold. Flake salmon into ½-inch pieces. Cook potatoes in pot of boiling salted water until just tender, about 10 minutes. Drain potatoes well; cool, peel and dice.

Whisk 5 tablespoons cream, 2 tablespoons horseradish and 2 tablespoons dill in small bowl until very thick. Whisk in vinegar. Season to taste with salt and pepper. Chill.

Mash ¾ cup diced potatoes, 1 tablespoon cream, 2 tablespoons horseradish and 1 tablespoon dill in medium bowl until almost smooth. Lightly mix in salmon, onions and remaining potatoes. Season with salt and pepper. Melt butter in heavy medium nonstick skillet over high heat. Add hash; press to compact. Reduce heat to medium and cook until bottom is brown and crusty, about 10 minutes. Using large spatula, turn over hash in sections. Press lightly and cook until bottom is brown, about 5 minutes. Turn out hash onto 2 plates. Serve with horseradish cream.

GERMANY'S HORSERADISH

German cooks have many tried-and-true ways of using horseradish in the kitchen. They create one condiment by grating the root and mixing it with vinegar, sugar and salt; they make another by combining the root with grated or sliced apple, which tempers the fire and produces a pleasant sweet-sour flavor. Horseradish can also be mixed with mustard, a natural pairing of two members of the crucifer family.

For some dishes, grated horseradish is added to cream sauce or whipped cream, sour cream or mayonnaise. Other, more elegant horseradish sauces might incorporate grated almonds or pistachios and be presented in a crystal dish.

Today you can buy fresh horseradish at many grocery stores, or you can even harvest it from your own garden; it grows tenaciously, like mint, yielding tender young leaves that are interesting in salads but are too perishable for the commercial market. And, of course, you can pick up the prepared version in the familiar jars at the supermarket.

Accompaniments

In kitchens all over the world–Asia and Latin America, Europe, Africa, the Middle East and the United States–cooks know that a simply prepared side dish can transform an ordinary meal into a feast. The following recipes can work that same culinary magic for you, whether you make French Baby Carrots with Tarragon or Chinese Chilled Asparagus with Sesame Vinaigrette, Italian Mushrooms Vittoria or Mexican "Drunken" Beans, Eastern European Challah or Italian Sage Focaccia.

Vegetables

CHILLED ASPARAGUS WITH SESAME VINAIGRETTE

8 SERVINGS

- 2 pounds asparagus, trimmed
- 2 tablespoons plus 2 teaspoons Oriental sesame oil
- 1 tablespoon plus 1 teaspoon rice vinegar
- 1 tablespoon plus 1 teaspoon soy sauce
- 1 teaspoon sugar
  Salt and pepper
  Sesame seeds, toasted

Cook asparagus in large skillet of boiling salted water until just crisp-tender, about 4 minutes. Drain. Rinse with cold water and drain well. Pat dry with paper towels. Arrange on platter. Mix sesame oil, rice vinegar, soy sauce and sugar in small bowl. Season dressing to taste with salt and pepper. (*Asparagus and dressing can be prepared 1 day ahead. Cover separately and refrigerate.*) Spoon dressing over asparagus. Sprinkle with sesame seeds and serve.

BABY CARROTS WITH TARRAGON

6 SERVINGS

- 4 bunches baby carrots (each about 8 ounces), peeled, trimmed, 3 inches of stems left intact
- ¼ cup water
- 3 tablespoons minced fresh tarragon or 3 teaspoons dried
- 2 tablespoons (¼ stick) butter
- 1 tablespoon white wine vinegar
- 1 tablespoon honey
  Salt and pepper

Combine carrots, ¼ cup water, 1½ tablespoons tarragon, butter, vinegar and honey in heavy large skillet. Bring to boil. Reduce heat to medium; cover and simmer until carrots are almost tender, about 12 minutes. Uncover; cook until carrots are tender and liquid is reduced to glaze, about 6 minutes longer. Season with salt and pepper. Transfer to platter. Sprinkle with 1½ tablespoons tarragon.

MEXICAN CORN

4 SERVINGS

- 3 tablespoons butter
- 1 10-ounce package frozen corn kernels, thawed
- 1 red bell pepper, chopped
- 1 cup chopped zucchini
- 2 green onions, chopped
- 1 jalapeño chili, seeded, chopped
- ½ cup purchased salsa
- 2 tablespoons chopped fresh cilantro

Melt butter in heavy large skillet over medium-high heat. Add corn, red bell pepper, zucchini, green onions and jalapeño and sauté until vegetables are tender, about 6 minutes. Mix in salsa and chopped cilantro. Stir until heated through, about 1 minute. Season to taste with salt and pepper.

MUSHROOMS VITTORIA

6 SIDE-DISH SERVINGS

2 tablespoons (¼ stick) butter
2 tablespoons olive oil
6 large garlic cloves, flattened
1¼ pounds large mushrooms, halved
    or quartered if very large
1 cup dry white wine
    Salt and pepper
    Chopped Italian parsley

Melt butter with oil in heavy large skillet over medium-high heat. Add garlic and sauté until beginning to brown, about 2 minutes. Using slotted spoon, remove garlic and discard. Add mushrooms and sauté until brown and juices evaporate, about 15 minutes. Add wine and simmer until reduced to glaze on mushrooms, stirring occasionally, about 10 minutes. Season mushrooms to taste with salt and pepper. Sprinkle with parsley and serve.

ENGLAND

POTATO, CELERY ROOT AND STILTON GRATIN

6 SERVINGS

2 pounds russet potatoes,
    unpeeled, thinly sliced
1 pound celery root (celeriac),
    peeled, halved, thinly sliced
2 cups low-salt chicken broth
1 cup whipping cream
3 large shallots, thinly sliced
½ teaspoon celery seeds
    Salt and pepper

2 cups crumbled Stilton cheese

Preheat oven to 400°F. Combine first 6 ingredients in heavy large skillet. Bring to simmer. Reduce heat to medium-low, cover and cook 10 minutes, turning vegetables occasionally.

Using slotted spoon, transfer half of vegetables to 9x13-inch baking dish. Season with salt and pepper. Sprinkle ¾ cup cheese over. Top with remaining vegetables. Pour cooking liquid over. Season with salt and pepper. Sprinkle ¾ cup cheese over. Cover with foil; bake 45 minutes. Uncover; sprinkle with remaining ½ cup cheese. Bake until liquid is almost absorbed, about 55 minutes. Cool 20 minutes before serving.

GRILLED CHILI CORN

Make sure you have lots of extra napkins on hand when you bring out this spicy grilled corn.

12 SERVINGS

½ cup olive oil
¼ cup fresh lime juice
2 tablespoons chili powder
1 teaspoon dried crushed red pepper
Salt
12 ears corn, husked

½ cup (1 stick) butter, melted

Prepare barbecue (medium-high heat). Combine first 4 ingredients in large bowl and whisk to blend. Season generously with salt. Place corn in large baking dish. Rub all of oil mixture over corn, covering completely.

Grill corn until tender, basting frequently with melted butter and any oil mixture from bottom of baking dish and turning frequently, about 10 minutes. Transfer to platter and serve.

Beans & Grains

"DRUNKEN" BEANS

Called frijoles borrachos *in Mexico, these beans are accented with dark beer.*

6 SERVINGS

8 bacon slices, cut into 1-inch pieces

1 pound dried pinto beans
5½ cups water
2 onions, chopped
8 large garlic cloves, minced
1 12-ounce bottle dark beer
4 teaspoons ground cumin
1 tablespoon ground coriander
1 tablespoon sugar
1 tablespoon chili powder
1 jalapeño chili, chopped

3 plum tomatoes, chopped
1 cup chopped fresh cilantro
Salt and pepper

Cook bacon in heavy large pot over medium-high heat until brown and almost crisp. Using slotted spoon, transfer to paper towels and drain; discard drippings. Return bacon to pot.

Place beans in same pot. Add water, onions and garlic; boil 15 minutes. Reduce heat to medium. Add beer, cumin, coriander, sugar, chili powder and jalapeño. Cover partially and simmer 1 hour.

Add tomatoes to beans, cover partially and simmer 45 minutes. Uncover; simmer until beans are tender and mixture is thick, about 20 minutes. (*Can be made 1 day ahead. Cover; chill. Bring to simmer before serving.*) Stir cilantro into beans. Season with salt and pepper.

BARLEY, CORN, RED PEPPER AND GREEN ONION PILAF

6 SERVINGS

1 tablespoon olive oil
1 large red bell pepper, chopped
2 bunches green onions, chopped
1½ cups pearl barley
2 14½-ounce cans vegetable broth

or chicken broth
2 cups frozen corn
½ cup sliced fresh basil
Salt and pepper

Heat oil in heavy medium saucepan over medium-high heat. Add chopped bell pepper and half of green onions and sauté until tender, about 5 minutes. Add barley and stir to coat with olive oil. Add vegetable broth and bring to boil, stirring occasionally. Reduce heat, cover and simmer until barley is tender, stirring occasionally, about 40 minutes. Add corn and stir until heated through, about 5 minutes. Mix in sliced basil and remaining green onions. Season to taste with salt and pepper and serve.

FRENCH COUNTRY VEGETABLES

For dishes full of the flavors, colors and aromas of French country gardens, don't miss *Roger Vergé's Vegetables in the French Style* (Artisan, 1994, $35).

MEXICO

SPICY BLACK BEANS WITH BELL PEPPERS AND RICE

8 SERVINGS

1 tablespoon vegetable oil
1 large onion, diced
1 cup chopped green bell pepper
1 cup chopped red bell pepper
3 large garlic cloves, chopped
1 tablespoon ground cumin
1 jalapeño chili, seeded, chopped
1 teaspoon dried oregano
2 15- to 16-ounce cans black beans, drained
2 cups canned crushed tomatoes with added puree
¼ cup orange juice
1½ teaspoons hot pepper sauce (such as Tabasco)
Salt and pepper

1⅓ cups raw rice, cooked

Heat oil in heavy large skillet over medium-high heat. Add onion, bell peppers, garlic, cumin, jalapeño and oregano; sauté until vegetables begin to soften, about 8 minutes. Mash ½ cup beans. Add mashed beans, whole beans, tomatoes, orange juice and hot pepper sauce to skillet. Bring to boil, stirring frequently. Reduce heat, cover and simmer 15 minutes. Uncover and simmer until reduced to thick sauce consistency, stirring occasionally, about 15 minutes. Season with salt and pepper.

Mound rice in center of platter. Spoon black bean mixture over.

WILD THING

Indigenous to Minnesota, wild rice is a delicacy that was first harvested by the Ojibwa Indians. The nutty-tasting organic wild rice from Manitok grows in lakes and rivers where it has been a crop of the Ojibwa for hundreds of years.

Breads

SAGE FOCACCIA

This stylish bread, with its roots on the Ligurian coast of Italy, is on tables everywhere these days. It's much easier to make than you might think, especially when you use frozen bread dough.

4 TO 6 SERVINGS

1 1-pound loaf frozen bread dough, thawed
6 tablespoons chopped fresh sage
3 tablespoons olive oil
  Pepper

¾ cup coarsely grated Pecorino Romano cheese (about 2¼ ounces)
  Fresh sage leaves

Place dough in medium bowl. Add 3 tablespoons chopped fresh sage, 1 tablespoon olive oil and generous amount of ground pepper. Knead in bowl to incorporate. Let dough rest 10 minutes.

Press out dough on generously floured surface to 12x9-inch oval. Transfer dough to ungreased baking sheet. Brush dough with 1 tablespoon olive oil. Let dough rise in warm draft-free area 30 minutes.

Preheat oven to 425°F. Lightly dimple dough all over with fingertips. Brush with remaining 1 tablespoon olive oil. Bake 10 minutes. Sprinkle dough with remaining 3 tablespoons chopped fresh sage, then grated Romano cheese. Bake bread until edges are brown, about 7 minutes longer. Serve bread hot, warm or at room temperature; garnish with fresh sage leaves.

CUMIN FLATBREAD

This bread is thin, chewy and fragrant with spice and citrus.

6 SERVINGS

1⅓ cups warm water (105°F to 115°F)
1 envelope dry yeast
3 tablespoons extra-virgin olive oil

1 tablespoon minced lemon peel (yellow part only)
2¼ teaspoons coarse salt
2 teaspoons ground cumin
3 cups bread flour

1 tablespoon cumin seeds
1 tablespoon sesame seeds

Place warm water in bowl of heavy-duty mixer. Sprinkle yeast over and stir to combine. Let stand 10 minutes. Add oil, lemon peel, salt and ground cumin. Using dough hook attachment, gradually beat in flour. Continue beating 5 minutes. Turn out dough onto lightly floured work surface and knead until smooth dough forms, about 2 minutes (dough will be very soft).

Lightly oil large bowl. Add dough; turn to coat. Cover with plastic and let rise in warm draft-free area until doubled in volume, about 1 hour.

Preheat oven to 400°F. Line 12x18-inch baking sheet with heavy-duty foil. Brush foil with oil. Place dough in pan. Using fingertips, press out dough, covering pan completely (dough will be very thin). Sprinkle with cumin seeds and sesame seeds. Bake until golden, about 30 minutes. Loosen bread from foil. Serve warm or at room temperature.

U.S.A.

CHEDDAR CORNMEAL MUFFINS

MAKES 12

1 cup all-purpose flour
1 cup white cornmeal
1 tablespoon baking powder
1 teaspoon salt
½ teaspoon baking soda
¼ teaspoon cayenne pepper
1 cup buttermilk
6 tablespoons unsalted butter, melted, cooled slightly
1 large egg
1 cup grated cheddar cheese

Preheat oven to 425°F. Line twelve ⅓-cup muffin cups with paper or foil liners. Stir first 6 ingredients in large bowl to blend. Whisk buttermilk, butter and egg in medium bowl to blend. Add to dry ingredients and stir just until combined. Fold in grated cheddar cheese.

Divide batter equally among prepared muffin cups. Bake muffins until tops are golden and tester inserted into center comes out clean, about 20 minutes. Cool in pan on rack 10 minutes. Serve warm or at room temperature.

ITALY

PORCINI, OLIVE AND ROSEMARY FOCACCIA

8 SERVINGS

1 ounce dried porcini mushrooms, reconstituted in 1 cup hot water (see recipe)
1 envelope dry yeast
¼ cup olive oil
2 teaspoons coarse salt
2 teaspoons chopped fresh rosemary
2 cups plus 4 tablespoons (about) unbleached all-purpose flour
½ cup coarsely chopped pitted brine-cured olives (such as Kalamata)

Add enough hot water to porcini soaking liquid to measure ¾ cup if necessary. Heat liquid in small saucepan to 105°F to 115°F. Pour into processor. Sprinkle yeast over. Let stand until yeast dissolves, about 12 minutes. Add oil, 1 teaspoon salt and 1 teaspoon rosemary. Process 3 seconds. Add 2 cups plus 2 tablespoons flour and process until moist clumps form, adding more flour if necessary. Mix in olives, using 4 on/of turns. Turn out dough into large bowl. Add porcini and knead until mixed in (dough will be firm and sticky).

Generously flour heavy large baking sheet. Turn out dough onto sheet. Using floured hands, press out dough to irregular 13x9-inch rectangle. Sprinkle dough with remaining 1 teaspoon salt and 1 teaspoon rosemary. Cover baking sheet with plastic wrap. Let dough rise in warm draft-free area until puffy, about 1 hour.

Preheat oven to 400°F. Bake bread until crusty, about 25 minutes. Serve warm or at room temperature.

RECONSTITUTED DRIED PORCINI

Here's how to reconstitute the dried porcini mushrooms in this recipe.

1 ounce dried porcini mushrooms
1 cup hot water

Combine porcini and water in medium bowl. Let stand until porcini soften, about 40 minutes. Pour mixture into strainer set over small bowl. Press porcini to release excess liquid. Coarsely chop porcini. Pour soaking liquid into measuring cup, leaving any sediment behind; reserve soaking liquid.

ITALY'S PRIZED PORCINI

Few subjects unite Italians in a stronger passion than the one that heats their blood during the season "of the pig," or *porcino*, as *Boletus edulis* is known. The mushrooms are found all over Europe—wherever there is moist, peaty soil in woods of chestnut, beech, birch, oak and pine.

The best, however, are said to come from three regions in Italy: the Ligurian Apennines; Calabria's chestnut groves on the Sila plateau; and the Dolomites' cool forests in Trentino-Alto Adige. Easier pickings are available at the markets on Turin's via Lagrange, a gastronomic Fifth Avenue, and in Trento's Piazza Lodron north of Lake Garda.

Porcini are hunted from late May to July, and again from September through November. During these months, strangers lurking near fungi hiding places are regarded with suspicion by experienced locals, who hope to gather as many as 50 to 60 pounds for commercial sun-drying, a long-established industry.

The *Boletus* genus (from *bolos*, the Greek word for "lump of earth") gets its bosky, meaty flavor from a high content of glutamic acid, making it the vegetable equivalent of MSG. This quality also gives porcini the power to intensify the savoriness of other ingredients.

These special mushrooms come at a price. Because they are not grown commercially, porcini are expensive. They do cost less when dried, which is how they are usually sold in the United States (typically at Italian markets, specialty foods stores and some supermarkets). Having lost 90 percent of their weight, dried porcini have a more intense flavor.

ALMOST GRANDMOTHER'S CHALLAH

To make this traditional Jewish bread easier to prepare, shape the dough into two loaves after the second rising instead of forming braided loaves, as is traditional. Place each loaf in a 9x5x3-inch loaf pan coated with nonstick vegetable spray and continue as per recipe.

MAKES 2 LOAVES

½ cup plus ⅔ cup warm water (105°F to 115°F)
2 tablespoons dry yeast
1 tablespoon plus ¾ cup sugar

5 large eggs
¾ cup vegetable oil
1 teaspoon salt
7½ cups (about) all-purpose flour

1 large egg yolk
1 tablespoon water

Combine ½ cup warm water, yeast and 1 tablespoon sugar in large glass measuring cup and stir until yeast dissolves. Let yeast mixture stand at room temperature until foamy, about 10 minutes.

In large bowl of heavy-duty mixer-fitted with whisk attachment, beat 5 eggs until blended. Add oil, salt and ¾ cup sugar and beat until pale yellow and slightly thickened, about 4 minutes. Beat in ⅔ cup warm water. Add yeast mixture and beat until blended. Remove whisk and fit mixer with dough hook. Add enough flour 1 cup at a time to form smooth dough, beating well after each addition. Beat on medium speed until smooth and elastic, about 5 minutes, adding flour by tablespoonfuls if sticky. Turn out onto floured surface and knead 2 minutes.

Lightly oil large bowl. Add dough, turning to coat with oil. Cover with plastic wrap, then with clean kitchen towel. Let dough rise in warm draft-free area until doubled in volume, about 1 hour.

Punch down dough. Cover with plastic and clean kitchen towel and let rise 30 minutes.

Grease 2 large baking sheets. Turn out dough onto lightly floured surface. Divide dough into 2 equal portions. Divide each portion into 3 equal pieces. Roll each piece into 9-inch-long rope. Braid 3 ropes together; pinch ends together to seal. Repeat with remaining dough pieces, forming 2 braids. Place each braid on baking sheet. Cover with towel. Let rise in warm area until almost doubled, about 30 minutes.

Preheat oven to 400°F. Whisk yolk with 1 tablespoon water to blend. Brush dough with egg mixture. Bake 10 minutes. Reduce oven temperature to 350°F. Bake until bread is golden brown and sounds hollow when tapped on bottom, about 35 minutes. Transfer loaves to rack and cool completely. (*Can be prepared 1 day ahead. Wrap tightly in plastic and store at room temperature.*)

BASIL, ROSEMARY AND TOMATO FOCACCIA

Fresh tomatoes and herbs top a delicious Italian bread. Accompany with the extra garlic oil.

MAKES 1 FOCACCIA

¾ cup olive oil
6 garlic cloves, minced
¾ teaspoon dried crushed red pepper
2 cups warm water (105°F to 115°F)
1 envelope dry yeast
5 cups (about) unbleached all-purpose flour
2 teaspoons salt

8 medium-size plum tomatoes, seeded, cut into 1-inch pieces
2 tablespoons coarse salt

2 tablespoons chopped fresh rosemary
2 tablespoons thinly sliced fresh basil

Combine oil, garlic and crushed red pepper in heavy small saucepan. Stir over medium-low heat until garlic is golden, about 5 minutes. Remove from heat and let stand at least 1 hour. *(Can be prepared 1 day ahead. Cover and refrigerate. Bring to room temperature before using.)*

Pour 2 cups warm water into large glass measuring cup. Sprinkle yeast over and let stand until yeast dissolves, about 10 minutes. Whisk in 3 tablespoons garlic oil. Combine 2 cups flour and 2 teaspoons salt in bowl of heavy-duty mixer. Add yeast mixture and beat until incorporated. Mix in enough remaining flour 1 cup at a time to form soft dough. Beat on low speed just until dough is smooth, about 3 minutes.

Brush large bowl with 1 tablespoon garlic oil. Transfer dough to prepared bowl. Turn to coat with oil. Cover with plastic, then damp kitchen towel. Let dough rise in warm draft-free area until doubled in volume, about 1 hour.

Place tomatoes in colander set over large bowl. Toss with 1 tablespoon coarse salt. Let stand 15 minutes. Rinse under cold water. Transfer tomatoes to paper towels; drain well.

Preheat oven to 450°F. Brush 15x10x1-inch baking sheet with 1 tablespoon garlic oil. Punch down dough. Knead briefly in bowl. Transfer dough to prepared sheet. Using oiled hands, stretch dough to roughly fit pan. Press dough all over with fingertips to dimple. Sprinkle dough with rosemary, then tomatoes, pressing some into dimples. Sprinkle with basil and remaining 1 tablespoon coarse salt.

Bake focaccia until golden brown, about 30 minutes. Transfer to rack. Cool. Cut focaccia into squares. Serve with remaining garlic oil.

Condiments

FRESH HORSERADISH WITH BEETS

A tangy condiment that's terrific with roast beef or corned beef. It also adds zip to Thousand Island dressing and is perfect alongside gefilte fish at Passover.

MAKES ABOUT 2 CUPS

2 cups ½-inch pieces peeled horseradish root (about 12 ounces before peeling)
¾ cup distilled white vinegar
½ cup finely chopped peeled raw beet
⅓ cup sugar
½ teaspoon coarse salt

Using processor fitted with shredder attachment, shred horseradish. Transfer horseradish to medium bowl. Fit processor with metal blade. Return horseradish to work bowl. Add next 3 ingredients. Process until almost smooth, scraping down sides of bowl occasionally, about 5 minutes. Mix in salt. Place horseradish in glass jar. Cover tightly; chill at least 1 day and up to 10 days.

NOPALITO SALSA

This unusual salsa calls for canned or bottled nopalitos, the stems of the prickly pear cactus. Available in the Mexican section of many supermarkets, they're sometimes labeled natural tender cactus. If you cannot find nopalitos at your local market, simply substitute cooked green beans. Use this tasty salsa as you would any other— with meats, chips and tacos.

MAKES ABOUT 2¼ CUPS

1⅓ cups canned or bottled nopalitos, rinsed, drained, diced (about one 11-ounce jar) or 1⅓ cups diced cooked green beans
¾ cup diced peeled jicama
2 small tomatoes, diced
⅓ cup diced onion
¼ cup chopped fresh cilantro
3 tablespoons red wine vinegar
1 tablespoon olive oil
1 serrano chili or small jalapeño chili, minced
1 garlic clove, minced
Salt and pepper

Combine all ingredients in medium bowl. Season to taste with salt and pepper. Cover and refrigerate until well chilled, about 2 hours. (*Can be prepared 6 hours ahead. Keep refrigerated.*)

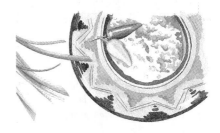

DOUBLE-BERRY PRESERVES

The fresh berries at the open-air markets of Nice inspired this simple recipe. The wide surface of a large skillet reduces the cooking time, which helps keep the fruit flavor at its peak.

MAKES 2 CUPS

2 1-pint baskets strawberries, hulled, diced
1 ½-pint basket fresh raspberries or 1½ cups frozen unsweetened, thawed
¾ cup sugar

Combine all ingredients in heavy large skillet. Stir over low heat until sugar dissolves. Increase heat and boil until preserves are very thick, stirring frequently, about 10 minutes. Spoon into small bowl. Cover and refrigerate. (*Can be prepared 1 week ahead. Keep refrigerated.*)

OLIVE OIL PLUS

The new "Flavored Oils Collection" from Colavita features their extra-virgin olive oils flavored with basil, lemon or pepper. The bottles sport original artwork on the labels; line them up on a kitchen counter to inspire your next culinary creation. For information, call 800-665-4731.

PICO DE GALLO

Offer this fresh salsa with tortilla chips as an appetizer.

MAKES ABOUT 5 CUPS

2¼ pounds plum tomatoes, seeded, finely chopped
1 large onion, finely chopped
¾ cup chopped fresh cilantro
5 garlic cloves, minced
3 jalapeño chilies, seeded, minced
3 tablespoons fresh lime juice
Salt and pepper

Combine all ingredients in bowl. Season with salt and pepper. Cover; chill at least 1 hour and up to 4 hours before serving.

Desserts

If food may be said to be an international language, then dessert is the dialect spoken most widely–and enthusiastically. Nothing excites the imagination quite like Italian Tiramisù, Moroccan Perfumed Oranges, American Apple-Cranberry Crisp, English Mincemeat Tartlets with Lemon Cream or the Simplest Chocolate Honey Mousse from France. Nothing you prepare is likely to win more raves than the recipes on the pages that follow–whatever language is spoken.

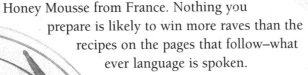

Fruit

APPLE-CRANBERRY CRISP

6 SERVINGS

1½ pounds tart green apples, peeled, cored, cut into ¾-inch pieces
3 cups fresh or frozen cranberries
⅔ cup sugar
4 tablespoons all-purpose flour
1 teaspoon ground cinnamon
½ teaspoon ground nutmeg

¾ cup old-fashioned rolled oats
2 tablespoons firmly packed golden brown sugar
3 tablespoons butter, cut into pieces, room temperature
Vanilla frozen yogurt

Preheat oven to 375°F. Toss apples, cranberries, ⅔ cup sugar, 2 tablespoons flour, cinnamon and nutmeg to blend in large bowl. Transfer to 8x8x2-inch glass baking dish. Let stand 15 minutes.

Combine oats, brown sugar and remaining 2 tablespoons flour in medium bowl. Add butter and stir until moist clumps form. Sprinkle topping over filling. Bake until topping is golden brown and filling bubbles, about 1 hour. Cool slightly. Serve warm or at room temperature with frozen yogurt.

CARIBBEAN

TROPICAL BANANA SUNDAES

4 SERVINGS

Vanilla ice cream or frozen yogurt

3 tablespoons unsalted butter
4 ripe but firm bananas, peeled, thickly sliced on diagonal
1 cup purchased chocolate sauce, warmed
Toasted sweetened coconut

Place 1 scoop vanilla ice cream in each of 4 dessert bowls. Place bowls in freezer.

Melt butter in heavy large skillet over medium heat. Add bananas; sauté until just beginning to soften, about 3 minutes. Spoon bananas over ice cream. Top with chocolate sauce and coconut.

MOROCCO

PERFUMED ORANGES

Orange blossom water provides the "perfume" in this simple dessert.

6 SERVINGS

6 navel oranges
⅓ cup honey
¼ cup orange juice
1 tablespoon orange blossom water*

1 teaspoon ground cinnamon
Mint sprigs (optional)

Using small sharp knife, cut peel and white pith from all oranges. Slice oranges into thin rounds. Arrange orange slices in shallow glass baking dish. Stir honey, orange juice and orange blossom water in heavy small saucepan over medium heat until honey melts. Pour honey mixture over orange slices. Refrigerate at least 1 hour and up to 4 hours, basting orange slices occasionally.

Arrange orange slices decoratively on large serving platter. Spoon honey sauce over. Sprinkle with ground cinnamon. Garnish orange slices with mint sprigs, if desired.

Sometimes called orange flower water, this extract is available at most liquor stores and in the liquor section of some supermarkets.

U.S.A.

FRUIT WITH CASSIS-SPIKED LEMON CURD SAUCE

There's no easier dessert than fresh fruit. But for something a little more spirited, top it with some store-bought lemon curd lightened with yogurt and flavored with crème de cassis.

4 SERVINGS

½ cup purchased lemon curd

2 tablespoons crème de cassis (black currant-flavored liqueur)
½ cup plain yogurt, crème fraîche or sour cream (not low-fat or nonfat)

3 oranges, peel and white pith removed, fruit sliced, slices quartered
1 1-pint basket strawberries, hulled, halved
Fresh mint sprigs

Whisk lemon curd and crème de cassis in small bowl to blend. Stir in yogurt. *(Sauce can be prepared 2 days ahead. Cover and refrigerate.)*

Combine oranges and strawberries in medium bowl. *(Can be prepared 6 hours ahead. Cover fruit and refrigerate.)* Spoon fruit into balloon glasses. Spoon lemon curd sauce over. Garnish with mint sprigs and serve.

Puddings & Mousses

SIMPLEST CHOCOLATE HONEY MOUSSE

Sweetening the mousse with honey adds a Provençal touch to a classic French dessert.

8 SERVINGS

2½ cups chilled whipping cream
12 ounces bittersweet (not unsweetened) or semisweet chocolate, chopped
5 tablespoons honey

Stir ¾ cup cream, chocolate and honey in heavy medium saucepan over low heat until chocolate melts and mixture is smooth. Cool, stirring occasionally.

In large bowl, beat 1¼ cups cream until soft peaks form. Fold cream into chocolate mixture in 2 additions. Divide mousse among eight ¾-cup ramekins.

Refrigerate until set, about 2 hours.

Whip remaining ½ cup cream to firm peaks. Spoon a dollop of cream in center of each mousse.

POACHED PEAR AND RASPBERRY TRIFLE WITH ORANGE CUSTARD

The first "trifles" were simply unadorned custards, but by Victorian times, they had become the sophisticated dessert we think of today—liquor-soaked cake layered with jam and custard and covered with whipped cream. This trifle is made with poached pears, raspberries, orange custard and pound cake.

16 SERVINGS

POACHED PEARS

1 750-ml bottle Johannisberg Riesling
¾ cup sugar
3¼ pounds Anjou pears, peeled, halved, cored
4 whole cloves
½ cup cream sherry

CUSTARD

10 large egg yolks
⅔ cup sugar
7 tablespoons cornstarch
4 cups half-and-half
¼ cup (½ stick) unsalted butter
1 tablespoon grated orange peel
2 teaspoons vanilla extract

1½ (about) 12-ounce purchased pound cakes

⅔ cup raspberry jam
5 ½-pint baskets raspberries

2 cups chilled whipping cream
2 tablespoons sugar
Fresh mint leaves

FOR PEARS: Bring wine and sugar to simmer in heavy large saucepan, stirring until sugar dissolves. Add pears and cloves and bring to boil. Reduce heat, cover and simmer until pears are just tender, turning occasionally, about 25 minutes. Using slotted spoon, transfer pears to plate and cool. Boil poaching liquid until reduced to ²/₃ cup syrup, about 20 minutes. Cool pear syrup. Mix in sherry. Thinly slice pears; drain on paper towels.

FOR CUSTARD: Whisk yolks, ²/₃ cup sugar and cornstarch in bowl. Bring half-and-half to simmer in heavy large saucepan. Gradually whisk hot half-and-half into yolk mixture. Return mixture to same saucepan. Whisk over medium heat until custard boils, about 8 minutes. Boil 1 minute, whisking constantly. Remove from heat. Pour into bowl. Add butter; whisk until melted. Whisk in orange peel and vanilla. Chill until cool, whisking occasionally, about 1 hour.

Cut cakes crosswise into ½-inch-thick slices. Cut each slice into 4 squares.

Arrange enough cake in bottom of 4-quart glass trifle dish or bowl to cover bottom. Brush cake with 1 tablespoon pear syrup, then spread 2 tablespoons jam over, allowing jam to show at sides of dish. Sprinkle with 1 cup raspberries, arranging some berries to show at sides of dish. Spread 1¼ cups custard over cake to cover, making sure

custard touches sides of dish. Top with single layer of sliced pears, arranging some to show at sides of dish. Arrange enough cake over to cover. Brush with 3 tablespoons syrup, then spread 4 tablespoons jam over. Sprinkle with 1½ cups berries. Spread 1½ cups custard over. Top with single layer of pears. Arrange enough cake cover to cover. Brush with 5 tablespoons syrup, then spread 5 tablespoons jam over. Sprinkle 1½ cups berries over. Spread remaining custard over. Place remaining pears decoratively atop dessert. *(Cover; chill at least 4 hours or overnight.)*

Whip cream and 2 tablespoons sugar in large bowl to medium peaks. Spoon cream into pastry bag fitted with star tip. Pipe large rosettes of cream around edge of dish. Garnish with remaining berries and mint leaves.

FROZEN HAZELNUT-TANGERINE TIRAMISÙ

As Italian restaurants continue to grow in popularity, so does tiramisù. *This version of the dessert, made of triple cream cheese from Italy* (mascarpone), *ladyfingers, espresso and cocoa powder, is updated by adding nuts and tangerine juice and serving it frozen.*

12 SERVINGS

PRALINE

½ cup sugar
¼ cup water
1 cup hazelnuts, toasted

FILLING

1 cup fresh tangerine juice
 (from about 5 tangerines)
1 cup plus 10 tablespoons sugar
8 large egg yolks
1 cup plus 10 tablespoons water
½ cup whipping cream
1 tablespoon grated tangerine peel
2 8.8-ounce containers mascarpone

cheese or 16 ounces whipped cream cheese

7 tablespoons Grand Marnier or other orange liqueur

5 teaspoons instant espresso powder or instant coffee powder

3 (about) 4.4-ounce packages Champagne biscuits (4-inch-long ladyfinger-like biscuits)

Unsweetened cocoa powder
Tangerine slices (optional)

FOR PRALINE: Lightly oil baking sheet. Stir sugar and water in heavy medium saucepan over medium heat until sugar dissolves. Increase heat and boil without stirring until syrup turns deep amber, brushing down sides of pan with pastry brush dipped into water and swirling pan occasionally. Mix in nuts. Pour onto prepared sheet; cool. Coarsely chop praline.

FOR FILLING: Boil tangerine juice in heavy large saucepan until reduced to ¼ cup, about 12 minutes. Set aside.

Whisk 1 cup sugar and yolks in large metal bowl. Whisk in 1 cup water. Set bowl over saucepan of simmering water and whisk constantly until candy thermometer registers 180°F, about 5 minutes. Remove from over water. Using electric mixer, beat mixture until cool, about 5 minutes. Mix in tangerine juice, cream and peel. Add mascarpone and 2 tablespoons Grand Marnier and beat until smooth. Fold in 1 cup praline (reserve remaining praline for another use). Chill filling while preparing biscuits.

Line 9-inch-diameter springform pan with 2¾-inch-high sides with plastic wrap. Stir remaining 10 tablespoons sugar, 10 tablespoons water and espresso powder in heavy small saucepan over low heat until sugar dissolves. Mix in 5 tablespoons Grand Marnier. Cool syrup.

Using sharp knife, trim 1 biscuit to 3-inch length. Soak biscuit in syrup 10 seconds per side. Place rounded end up and sugared side against side of pre-

pared pan. Repeat with as many biscuits as necessary to cover sides of pan. Soak more biscuits in syrup and place on bottom of pan, covering completely. Pour half of filling into pan. Soak more biscuits in syrup 10 seconds per side; place atop filling, covering completely. Spoon remaining filling over. Freeze overnight.

Release pan sides from cake. Fold down plastic. Sift cocoa over dessert. Garnish with tangerine slices, if desired.

SHORTCUT TIRAMISÙ

A cross between cheesecake and trifle, this Italian dessert is ideal for a crowd because it serves a lot of people, it is completed a day ahead—and everyone loves it. The version below is nice for a busy cook because the cake is made from a packaged mix; turn the remaining half of the batter into cupcakes. Even easier: If there's a local bakery you like, pick up a nine-inch-diameter sponge cake to use as the base.

10 TO 12 SERVINGS

1 18½-ounce package Duncan Hines Moist Deluxe Butter Recipe Golden Cake Mix

6 large egg yolks
½ cup plus 3 tablespoons sugar
⅔ cup dry Marsala

2 8-ounce packages cream cheese, room temperature
½ cup sour cream
1 cup chilled whipping cream

½ cup water
2½ teaspoons instant espresso powder
2 tablespoons coffee liqueur
½ cup grated semisweet chocolate

Preheat oven to 350°F. Butter and flour 9-inch-diameter cake pan with 1½-inch-high sides. Prepare cake mix according to package directions. Pour half of batter (about 3 cups) into prepared pan; bake remaining batter as cupcakes. Bake until tester inserted into center of cake comes out clean, about 20 minutes. Transfer to rack and cool 10 minutes. Invert cake onto rack and cool completely.

Whisk yolks and ½ cup sugar in top of double boiler. Gradually whisk in Marsala. Whisk over boiling water until mixture triples in volume and thermometer registers 160°F, about 4 minutes. Remove top of double boiler from over water. Cool Marsala mixture to room temperature, whisking occasionally.

Using electric mixer, beat cream cheese and sour cream in large bowl until fluffy. Gradually beat in Marsala mixture. Using electric mixer with clean dry beaters, beat cream and 2 tablespoons sugar in medium bowl until stiff peaks form. Gently fold whipped cream into cheese mixture in 2 additions.

Stir water, espresso powder, coffee liqueur and remaining 1 tablespoon sugar in small bowl until espresso and sugar dissolve. Using serrated knife, cut cake in half horizontally. Brush cut side of 1 half with ¼ of espresso mixture. Place espresso side down in 9-inch-diameter glass soufflé dish. Brush top of cake in dish with ¼ of espresso mixture. Spread cheese mixture over cake. Brush cut side of remaining cake piece with ¼ of espresso mixture. Place espresso side down atop cheese mixture. Brush top of cake with remaining espresso mixture. Sprinkle chocolate over cake. Cover and refrigerate overnight.

Cakes

FLOURLESS LEMON-ALMOND CAKE

Almond and citrus trees cover Majorca's landscape, so it's no surprise that this cake, called gató, is offered in restaurants all over Palma. It is usually topped with homemade almond ice cream or ice, but purchased almond ice cream can also be used.

8 SERVINGS

1⅓ cups blanched slivered almonds
8 tablespoons sugar
4 large eggs, separated
5 teaspoons packed grated lemon peel
½ teaspoon ground cinnamon
Pinch of salt

Preheat oven to 375°F. Butter and flour 9-inch-diameter cake pan with 1½-inch-high sides. Line bottom of pan with waxed paper. Finely grind almonds with 2 tablespoons sugar in processor.

Combine yolks, 2 tablespoons sugar, lemon peel, cinnamon and salt in medium bowl. Using electric mixer, beat until thick and smooth, about 2 minutes. Stir in almond mixture. Using clean beaters, beat egg whites in large bowl until soft peaks form. Gradually add 4 tablespoons sugar, beating until stiff but not dry. Fold large spoonful of whites into almond mixture. Gently fold in remaining whites.

Transfer batter to pan. Bake until tester inserted into center comes out clean, about 35 minutes. Cool in pan on rack. Turn out onto platter. Remove waxed paper.

SOUR CREAM CHEESECAKE

This smooth, creamy cheesecake is a big, old-fashioned crowd pleaser. Make it a day before, because it needs to chill in the refrigerator overnight. For a pretty decoration, garnish the cheesecake with orange slices and mint sprigs.

12 SERVINGS

CRUST

2 cups graham cracker crumbs
½ cup walnuts (about 2 ounces)
¼ cup packed golden brown sugar
2 teaspoons ground cinnamon
7 tablespoons butter, melted

FILLING

3 8-ounce packages cream cheese, room temperature
1 cup sugar
Pinch of salt
1 16-ounce container sour cream
2 teaspoons grated orange peel
1 teaspoon vanilla extract
3 large eggs

FOR CRUST: Preheat oven to 350°F. Wrap outside of 9-inch-diameter springform pan with 2¾-inch-high sides with foil. Finely grind cracker crumbs, nuts, sugar and cinnamon in processor. Add butter and process until moist crumbs form. Press crust onto bottom and 2¼ inches up sides of pan. Bake crust until beginning to brown, about 15 minutes. Cool. Maintain oven temperature.

FOR FILLING: Blend cream cheese, sugar and salt in processor until smooth, stopping occasionally to scrape down sides. Add sour cream, orange peel and vanilla; process until well blended. Add eggs; blend until combined. Pour into crust. Bake until center no longer moves when pan is shaken and edges puff slightly, about 1 hour 5 minutes. Transfer to rack. Gently cut around pan sides to loosen crust. Place hot cheesecake directly in refrigerator; chill overnight.

Release pan sides from cake. Transfer cake to platter and serve.

SICILIAN MARZIPAN

Marzipan is a mixture of almond paste, sugar and egg whites. The extremely pliable confection can be rolled into thin sheets and used as a smooth, molded cover or wrapping for cakes; it can be cut into strips to form ribbons or other cake decorations; or it can be tinted and fashioned into a variety of shapes—like fruits, vegetables and animals.

The Sicilian tradition of making marzipan began during the Arab occupation of the island (a.d. 827-1040). In addition to introducing sugarcane and sugar-milling techniques to the Sicilians, the Arabs also shared their confectionery expertise. Since there was an abundance of almond trees on the island, marzipan became a very popular local treat.

According to Mary Taylor Simeri in *Pomp and Sustenance* (Knopf, 1989), the specialty of fruit-shaped marzipan comes from a Sicilian convent called the Monastery of the Martorana, founded in 1146.

As the story goes, the mother superior decided to play a prank on the archbishop, who was paying a visit during Easter. She instructed her nuns, who had become quite skilled at making marzipan, to mold the confection into realistically colored and shaped fruits, which were hung from the trees on the convent grounds.

The "fruits" were so impressive that the tradition has since spread to pastry shops throughout Sicily and beyond. To this day, residents of Palermo, the capital city of Sicily, call fruit-shaped marzipan *frutta di Martorana*.

KIRSCH AND DRIED CHERRY KUGELHUPF

Orchards cover the landscape of Alsace and Lorraine, supplying the fruit for one of the area's most important products: eaux-de-vie, or fruit brandies. Kirsch, made from cherries and their pits, is the most common. It is often used to soak this traditional Alsatian breakfast yeast bread.

10 TO 12 SERVINGS

CAKE

1 cup dried tart cherries
½ cup golden raisins
4 tablespoons kirsch (clear cherry brandy)
¼ cup warm water (105°F to 115°F)
  Pinch of sugar
2 envelopes dry yeast
8 tablespoons (1 stick) unsalted butter, room temperature
¾ cup sugar
4 large egg yolks
1 tablespoon grated lemon peel
2 teaspoons vanilla extract
1 teaspoon almond extract
1 teaspoon salt
¾ cup lukewarm milk
3½ cups all-purpose flour

1 cup almonds, toasted, finely chopped

GLAZE

1 cup powdered sugar
2 tablespoons kirsch
2 teaspoons milk

FOR CAKE: Combine first 3 ingredients in medium bowl. Let stand 15 minutes.

Combine ¼ cup warm water and pinch of sugar in bowl. Sprinkle yeast over; stir to dissolve. Let stand 10 minutes.

Meanwhile, in large mixer bowl fitted with dough hook, beat 6 tablespoons butter, ¾ cup sugar, yolks, peel, vanilla, almond extract and salt until well blended. Add yeast mixture, milk and 1 cup flour and beat until smooth. Beat in dried fruits and their soaking liquid. Gradually add remaining 2½ cups flour and beat until very soft dough forms, about 6 minutes. Let stand 15 minutes.

Butter 12-cup kugelhupf or Bundt pan with 2 tablespoons butter. Add almonds; tilt pan to coat bottom and sides. Spoon dough into pan. Cover with plastic and towel. Let dough rise in warm place until within 1 inch of top of pan, about 2½ hours.

Preheat oven to 350°F. Bake kugelhupf until tester inserted into center comes out clean, about 35 minutes. Let stand 10 minutes. Turn out onto rack; cool completely.

FOR GLAZE: Combine sugar and kirsch in bowl. Add milk; stir. Spoon over kugelhupf.

DRY GOODS

With their chewy texture and concentrated natural sweetness, dried figs and apricots from Turkey make a healthful and tasty snack anytime. When chopped, they're a nice addition to stuffings, homemade breads and oatmeal cookies. Call Russ & Daughters at 212-475-4880 to order.

CHOCOLATE CHIP AND GINGER FROZEN YOGURT CAKE

Frozen yogurt has become the fashionable alternative to ice cream for those who crave the cool without all the calories or cholesterol. It has seldom tasted–or looked–better than it does in this dessert.

10 SERVINGS

CRUST

1½ cups gingersnap cookie crumbs
1 cup slivered almonds
    (about 4½ ounces), toasted
¼ cup packed brown sugar
5 tablespoons butter, melted

FILLING

2 pints vanilla frozen yogurt,
    softened slightly
1 pint chocolate frozen yogurt,
    softened slightly
6 ounces bittersweet (not
    unsweetened) or semisweet
chocolate, chopped into
    medium-fine pieces
¼ cup plus 2 tablespoons chopped
    drained stem ginger in syrup*
3 tablespoons syrup from stem
    ginger in syrup
6 tablespoons gingersnap cookie
    crumbs
1 jar purchased hot fudge sauce

FOR CRUST: Preheat oven to 325°F. Butter 9-inch-diameter springform pan with 2¾-inch-high sides. Combine gingersnap crumbs, almonds and brown sugar in processor and grind finely. Mix in butter. Transfer to prepared pan and press crumbs onto bottom and 2 inches up sides. Bake until golden, about 12 minutes. Cool completely on rack.

FOR FILLING: Turn vanilla frozen yogurt into large bowl. Turn chocolate frozen yogurt into medium bowl. Mix ⅔ cup chopped chocolate, ¼ cup ginger and 2 tablespoons ginger syrup into vanilla frozen yogurt. Mix remaining chopped chocolate, 2 tablespoons ginger and 1 tablespoon ginger syrup into chocolate frozen yogurt.

Spread half of vanilla frozen yogurt mixture in crust. Sprinkle with 2 tablespoons gingersnap crumbs. Spread chocolate frozen yogurt mixture over. Sprinkle with 2 tablespoons crumbs. Spread remaining vanilla frozen yogurt mixture over. Smooth top. Sprinkle remaining 2 tablespoons crumbs over. Freeze until firm, at least 2 hours.

Heat ¼ cup hot fudge sauce in heavy small saucepan over low heat until just warm. Drizzle decoratively over top of frozen yogurt cake. (*Can be prepared 2 days ahead. Cover and freeze.*)

Heat remaining hot fudge sauce in heavy small saucepan over low heat until warm. Cut cake into slices, spooning fudge sauce over each.

Stem ginger in syrup is sold in specialty foods stores and some supermarkets.

Caramel-Glazed Walnut Cake

The stately walnut tree is found all along the Isère Valley in the Dauphiné. The best, from Grenoble, are exported all over the world; look for a red label for proof of origin.

8 SERVINGS

CAKE
8 1-inch-thick slices French bread, crust trimmed, bread cut into cubes

1½ cups walnuts, lightly toasted

1 cup sugar
4 large egg yolks
2 tablespoons dark rum
4 teaspoons instant espresso coffee powder dissolved in 1 teaspoon water
1 teaspoon grated lemon peel
6 large egg whites
Pinch of salt

CARAMEL
½ cup sugar
2 tablespoons water

8 walnut halves, toasted

FOR CAKE: Preheat oven to 350°F. Butter 9-inch-diameter springform pan. Line bottom with parchment paper. Butter parchment. Dust pan with flour. Finely grind bread in processor. Spread on baking sheet. Bake until golden, stirring occasionally, about 10 minutes. Finely grind breadcrumbs in processor. Measure ¾ cup crumbs (reserve remainder for another use). Finely grind nuts in processor.

Using electric mixer, beat ¾ cup sugar and yolks in large bowl until thick, about 3 minutes. Beat in rum, coffee powder mixture and peel. Mix in ¾ cup crumbs and ground nuts. Beat whites and salt in another large bowl until soft peaks form. Gradually add remaining ¼ cup sugar and beat until stiff. Fold ⅓ of whites into batter. Fold in remaining whites in 2 additions.

Spoon batter into pan. Bake cake until tester inserted into center comes out clean, about 45 minutes. Cool in pan on rack 10 minutes. Turn out cake. Peel off parchment. Turn cake over; cool on rack 15 minutes.

Line baking sheet with foil. Lightly oil foil. Place cake on prepared sheet.

FOR CARAMEL: Combine sugar and water in heavy medium saucepan. Stir over medium-low heat until sugar dissolves. Increase heat to medium-high and boil without stirring until mixture turns amber, brushing down sides of pan with wet pastry brush and swirling pan occasionally, about 6 minutes. Pour caramel over top of cake. Oil tip of knife. Immediately cut through caramel layer only, marking 8 serving pieces. Garnish with walnut halves. Cool completely.

Tarts & Pastries

MOROCCO

ORANGE BLOSSOM ALMOND PASTRIES

Because of their crescent shape, these tender, filled pastries are called "gazelle horns" in Morocco. They have an almond paste center and are lightly scented with orange blossom water, an ingredient often used in Middle Eastern cooking.

MAKES 32

PASTRY
2 cups all-purpose flour
¼ teaspoon salt
1 cup (2 sticks) chilled unsalted butter, cut into small pieces
¼ cup (about) ice water

FILLING
½ cup blanched almonds, toasted
1 7-ounce package almond paste
¼ cup unsalted butter, room temperature
2 tablespoons sugar
1 large egg
3 tablespoons orange blossom water*

½ cup powdered sugar

FOR PASTRY: Combine flour and salt in large bowl. Add butter and rub with fingertips until mixture resembles coarse meal. Add enough ice water by tablespoonfuls just to bind dough, tossing mixture with fork. Divide dough into 2 pieces. Lightly dust dough with flour and flatten each piece into rectangle. Wrap in plastic and refrigerate at least 1 hour.

FOR FILLING: Finely grind almonds in processor. Add almond paste, butter, 2 tablespoons sugar, egg and 1 tablespoon orange blossom water. Process until smooth. Transfer to small bowl

and refrigerate 1 hour.

Position rack in center of oven and preheat to 400°F. Roll out 1 pastry rectangle on lightly floured surface to 13x15-inch rectangle. Trim to 12-inch square. Cut into sixteen 3-inch squares. Place 1 teaspoon filling ½ inch from 1 corner of 1 pastry square. Beginning at same corner, roll corner of dough tightly over filling and continue rolling as for jellyroll. Pinch ends firmly to seal in filling. Gently shape into crescent. Place crescent on large baking sheet. Repeat with remaining dough squares and filling. Roll, cut, fill and shape remaining pastry rectangle. Bake until golden brown, about 20 minutes. Cool slightly.

While pastries are still warm, brush lightly with remaining 2 tablespoons orange blossom water. Turn pastries 1 at a time in powdered sugar to coat. Transfer to rack and cool completely. (*Can be made 1 day ahead. Store in airtight container at room temperature.*)

*Sometimes called orange flower

water, this extract is available at most liquor stores and in the liquor section of some supermarkets.

NECTARINE AND RASPBERRY CROSTATA WITH VANILLA CRÈME FRAÎCHE

This Italian-style, free-form tart has buttery pastry and lots of fresh fruit.

8 SERVINGS

2 cups all-purpose flour
¼ cup sugar
½ teaspoon salt
1 cup (2 sticks) chilled unsalted
   butter
2 tablespoons (about) ice water

1 ½-pint basket raspberries
4 nectarines (about 1¼ pounds),
   pitted, thinly sliced
⅓ cup plus 2 tablespoons sugar
1 tablepoon fresh lemon juice

1 egg, beaten to blend

Vanilla Crème Fraîche
(see recipe)

Mix flour, ¼ cup sugar and salt in a processor. Add butter; using on/off pulses, process until mixture resembles coarse meal. Add water by tablespoonfuls and process just until moist clumps form. Gather dough into ball. Flatten into disk. Wrap in plastic and chill at least 1 hour. (*Can be made 1 day ahead. Keep chilled. Let soften slightly before rolling.*) Preheat oven to 375°F. Roll out dough on lightly floured parchment paper to ¼-inch-thick round. Trim dough to 14-inch round. Transfer parchment with dough to large baking sheet. Mash ½ cup raspberries in large bowl. Add remaining raspberries, nectarines, ⅓ cup sugar and lemon juice; toss to coat. Spoon mixture into center of dough, leaving 3-inch border. Sprinkle fruit with 2 tablespoons sugar. Fold border over fruit, pinching to seal any cracks. Brush dough with some of beaten egg.

Bake crostata until pastry is golden brown and filling bubbles, about 35 minutes. Transfer baking sheet to rack and cool crostata slightly.

Serve crostata warm or at room temperature with Vanilla Crème Fraîche.

VANILLA CRÈME FRAÎCHE

MAKES ABOUT 1 CUP

1 8-ounce container crème fraîche
   or sour cream
½ vanilla bean, split lengthwise
4½ teaspoons sugar

Place crème fraîche in medium bowl. Scrape seeds from vanilla bean into crème fraîche. Stir in sugar. Cover; refrigerate 1 hour. (*Can be prepared 3 days ahead. Keep refrigerated.*)

PINE NUT, HONEY AND ANISE TART

In the Mediterranean, pine nuts, honey and anise are commonly found in either sweet or savory dishes. Here the three ingredients come together in an unusual, easy-to-make tart. Be sure to thaw both packaged pie crusts; use one to repair any cracks that appear in the tart crust during baking.

8 SERVINGS

1 15-ounce package refrigerated pie crusts, room temperature
1 teaspoon all-purpose flour

½ cup honey
½ cup sugar
1 egg, beaten to blend
3 tablespoons anisette (anise-flavored liqueur)
1 teaspoon aniseed, ground in mortar with pestle
¼ teaspoon salt

5 tablespoons unsalted butter, melted
1 cup pine nuts

Preheat oven to 450°F. Unfold 1 crust and peel off plastic. Press out fold lines. If crust cracks, wet fingers and push edges together. Sprinkle crust with flour and, using fingers, spread flour over entire crust. Place crust floured side down in 9-inch-diameter tart pan with removable bottom. Fold overhang in and build up crust edges about ¼ inch above rim of pan. Pierce crust all over with fork. Bake until light brown, about 12 minutes. Patch any cracks in crust using second crust, if necessary. Cool on rack. Reduce oven temperature to 350°F.

Mix honey, sugar, egg, anisette, aniseed and salt in medium bowl. Stir in butter and nuts. Pour mixture into crust. Bake until top is dark brown (filling will set as it cools), about 40 minutes. Cool on rack. (*Can be made 8 hours ahead. Let stand at room temperature.*)

CRUSADING DESSERT

Panforte di Siena was baked during the Crusades, fortifying soldiers on their long journeys (*panforte* is Italian for "strong bread"). Today, Coffaro's Baking Company has its own version of this time-honored sweet. The chewy confection is laced with almonds, hazelnuts, candied fruits and honey, then dipped into semi-sweet chocolate. Call 800-242-4420 for more information.

PINE NUTS, PIÑONS AND PIGNOLIAS

Pine nuts, as the name suggests, are the seeds of the pine tree. But only about a dozen species of pine produce nuts whose size and flavor make them worth harvesting. Of these, the two most highly regarded are the slender, creamy white pignolia from the European stone pine and the smaller, darker, oval piñon from the piñon pine of the southwestern United States.

In Europe, the trees are grown on plantations. The cones are knocked from the branches with a long pole and set in the sun until the heat opens the scales that hold the seeds. Then the cones are either threshed by machine or hand-beaten to dislodge the seeds. Afterward, a thin shell remains, which is then removed by machine.

In the United States, the nuts are gathered in the wild. And while machines are available to assist in the harvest, hand picking is still the norm.

In classically prepared Southwest cooking, the native piñon nut is used, but the harvests are generally small, and vary quite a bit in yield from year to year. The nut most commonly found in stores and in restaurant dishes is the more readily available (and less expensive) European pignolia.

MINCEMEAT TARTLETS WITH LEMON CREAM

Early recipes for this classic Christmas pie called for meat as an ingredient, but it was later omitted and only fruits, nuts and spices were used. This version is made with tender pastry (reserve any extra for cookies) and a mincemeat of apple, dried cranberries, fruit peel and spices.

6 SERVINGS

CRUST
3¾ cups all-purpose flour
¾ cup sugar
1½ teaspoons grated lemon peel
1½ cups (3 sticks) chilled unsalted
   butter, cut into pieces
3 large egg yolks
4½ teaspoons (about) lemon juice

FILLING
1 8-ounce Granny Smith apple,
   peeled, cored, finely chopped
¾ cup dried cranberries or raisins
   (about 3 ounces)

½ cup (generous) chopped pecans
(about 2½ ounces)
½ cup chopped mixed dried candied
fruit peel (about 3 ounces)
½ cup packed golden brown sugar
¼ cup (½ stick) unsalted butter,
cut into small pieces
¼ cup dark rum
1 teaspoon ground cinnamon
¾ teaspoon ground allspice
½ teaspoon ground nutmeg
¼ teaspoon ground ginger

1 egg, beaten to blend (glaze)
Lemon Cream (see recipe)

FOR CRUST: Combine first 3 ingredients
in processor. Add butter; cut in using
on/off turns until mixture resembles
coarse meal. Add yolks and enough
juice by teaspoonfuls to form dough
that begins to clump together. Gather
dough into ball; flatten into disk. Wrap
in plastic; chill until firm, about 30
minutes. (*Can be made 1 day ahead.
Keep chilled. Let dough soften slightly
before rolling.*)

FOR FILLING: Mix first 11 ingredients in large bowl. (*Can be prepared 6
hours ahead. Cover with plastic wrap
and let stand at room temperature.*)

Preheat oven to 375°F. Roll out
dough on floured surface to ⅛-inch-
thick round. Cut out six 6-inch-
diameter rounds. Place each round in
4½-inch-diameter tartlet pan with ¾-
inch-high sides and removable bottom. Press dough into pans, leaving
overhang. Gather scraps; reroll to cut
out six 5-inch-diameter rounds and
at least 6 leaf shapes.

Spoon filling into crusts, dividing
equally. Place dough rounds atop
tartlets. Fold pastry edges together,
crimping to seal. Top with leaf cutouts.
Brush pastry with egg glaze. Set tartlets
directly onto oven rack. Bake until
golden, about 35 minutes. Cool completely. Gently press up tart pan bottoms to loosen crusts. Remove tartlets.
(*Can be made 1 day ahead. Cover and let
stand at room temperature.*) Serve with
Lemon Cream.

LEMON CREAM

MAKES ABOUT 1½ CUPS

¾ cup chilled whipping cream
2 tablespoons sugar
2 teaspoons grated lemon peel

Beat all ingredients in medium bowl to
soft peaks. Serve with tartlets.

Cookies

NO-FAIL CHOCOLATE CHIPPERS

MAKES ABOUT 2 DOZEN

2 cups old-fashioned rolled oats
1¾ cups all-purpose flour
1 teaspoon baking soda
½ teaspoon salt

½ cup (1 stick) butter, room
    temperature
1 cup (packed) golden brown sugar
½ cup sugar
2 large eggs
1 teaspoon vanilla extract
1 cup chopped walnuts
1 11.5-ounce package (about 2
    cups) milk chocolate chips

Preheat oven to 375°F. Finely grind oats in processor. Add flour, baking soda and salt and blend 5 seconds.

Beat butter and both sugars in large bowl until well blended. Beat in eggs and vanilla. Mix in dry ingredients. Mix in walnuts and chocolate chips.

For each cookie, form 2 rounded tablespoons dough into ball and place on ungreased baking sheet; flatten slightly. Bake until edges are golden brown, about 12 minutes. Cool on sheets 5 minutes. Transfer to racks; cool completely.

MIDDLE EAST

ORANGE WALNUT COOKIES

Try the more traditional orange flower water or rose water instead of the orange peel and juice concentrate to flavor these crispy cookies.

MAKES ABOUT 24

½ cup (1 stick) chilled unsalted
    butter or margarine, cut into
    pieces
¾ cup sugar
1 tablespoon frozen orange juice
    concentrate, thawed
1½ teaspoons grated orange peel
½ teaspoon vanilla extract
1½ cups self-rising flour

24 walnut halves (about)

Preheat oven to 325°F. Grease heavy large baking sheet. Blend butter in processor until smooth. Add sugar and process until fluffy. Mix in orange concentrate, orange peel and vanilla. Add flour and process just until dough comes together, scraping down sides of work bowl occasionally.

Form 1 rounded tablespoon of dough into ball. Place on prepared sheet; flatten to 2-inch round. Repeat with remaining dough. Press 1 walnut half firmly onto each round. Bake cookies until just beginning to color, about 12 minutes. Transfer cookies to racks and cool. (*Can be made 2 days ahead. Store in airtight container at room temperature.*)

CINNAMON-RAISIN BISCOTTI

These crisp, low-fat cookies are just right for dipping into dessert wine or cappuccino.

MAKES ABOUT 2 DOZEN

1 large egg
½ cup sugar
1 tablespoon brandy
1 teaspoon vanilla extract
¾ cup plus 2 tablespoons all-purpose flour
¾ teaspoon baking powder
¾ teaspoon ground cinnamon
¼ teaspoon (generous) salt
⅓ cup raisins
⅓ cup whole almonds, toasted

Preheat oven to 375°F. Lightly grease heavy large baking sheet. Using hand-held electric mixer, beat egg and sugar in medium bowl until very thick and fluffy, about 2 minutes. Beat in brandy and vanilla. Sift flour, baking powder, cinnamon and salt into egg mixture and blend well. Mix in raisins and almonds. Spoon dough onto prepared sheet to form 10- to 11-inch strip. Using moistened fingertips, shape dough into neat 11-inch-long by 2½-inch- wide log.

Bake until log just begins to brown and feels firm to touch, about 20 minutes. Cool cookie log on sheet 15 minutes. Maintain oven temperature.

Transfer cookie log to work surface. Using serrated knife, cut crosswise into ⅓-inch-wide slices. Arrange slices on same baking sheet. Bake 10 minutes. Turn slices over. Bake until beginning to color, about 8 minutes longer. Cool cookies completely on baking sheet (cookies will become very crisp). (*Can be prepared 1 week ahead. Store in airtight container at room temperature.*)

ALMOND-CHOCOLATE MACAROONS

MAKES 25

2 cups (about 9½ ounces) whole almonds, toasted
1 cup sugar
¼ teaspoon ground cinnamon
⅛ teaspoon salt
1 large egg
1 large egg white
¼ teaspoon almond extract
¾ cup finely chopped bittersweet (not unsweetened) or semisweet chocolate

Position rack in center of oven and preheat to 350°F. Line 2 heavy large baking sheets with foil. Butter foil and dust with flour. Finely grind almonds, sugar, cinnamon and salt in processor. Add egg, egg white and almond extract and process until mixture holds together. Transfer to bowl. Stir in chocolate.

Using moistened hands, roll mixture into 1-inch balls and place on prepared sheets. Flatten to ⅓-inch-thick rounds. Bake macaroons until tops puff and centers are still soft, about 12 minutes. Transfer to rack and cool completely. Store in airtight container at room temperature. (*Can be prepared 3 days ahead.*)

GINGER ALMOND WAFERS

MAKES ABOUT 26

1½ cups powdered sugar
1¼ cups all-purpose flour
 ½ cup (1 stick) chilled unsalted
    butter, diced
 1 tablespoon minced peeled fresh
    ginger
 1 tablespoon ground ginger
 ½ teaspoon ground cinnamon
 ½ teaspoon salt
 ¾ cup whole almonds, toasted
 3 tablespoons whipping cream
 3 tablespoons chopped
    crystallized ginger
    Powdered sugar

Preheat oven to 325°F. Line 2 heavy large baking sheets with parchment paper. Combine first 7 ingredients in processor and blend using on/off turns until mixture resembles coarse meal. Add almonds, cream and crystallized ginger and process just until moist clumps form. Shape dough into 1¼-inch-diameter balls. Place on prepared sheets. Moisten bottom of glass; dip into powdered sugar and press each dough ball to ¼-inch thickness.

Bake cookies until brown on bottom and at edges, about 28 minutes. Transfer cookies to rack and cool. (*Store airtight at room temperature.*)

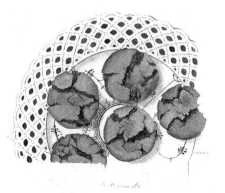

ORANGE AND CINNAMON BISCOTTI

The popularity of biscotti doesn't seem to end. These crunchy Italian cookies which are not too sweet or too rich, are the perfect finale to a contemporary meal. Serve them with sliced pears, espresso and Vin Santo, an Italian dessert wine, for a real treat. Enjoy leftovers with afternoon coffee or tea.

MAKES ABOUT 2 DOZEN

 1 cup sugar
 ½ cup (1 stick) unsalted butter,
    room temperature
 2 large eggs
 2 teaspoons grated orange peel
 1 teaspoon vanilla extract
 2 cups all-purpose flour
1½ teaspoons baking powder
 1 teaspoon ground cinnamon
 ¼ teaspoon salt

Preheat oven to 325°F. Butter 2 baking sheets. Beat sugar and butter in large bowl until blended. Add eggs 1 at a time, beating well after each. Beat in orange peel and vanilla. Stir flour, baking powder, cinnamon and salt into medium bowl. Add dry ingredients to butter mixture; mix just until incorporated.

Divide dough in half. Place each half on prepared sheet. With lightly floured hands, form each half into 3-inch-wide by ¾-inch-high log. Bake until dough logs are firm to touch, about 35 minutes. Remove dough logs from oven and cool 10 minutes.

Transfer logs to work surface. Using serrated knife, cut on diagonal into ½-inch-thick slices. Arrange cut side down on baking sheets. Bake until bottoms are golden, about 12 minutes. Turn biscotti over; bake until bottoms are golden, about 12 minutes longer. Transfer to racks and cool. (*Can be made 2 weeks ahead. Store in airtight container.*)

INDEX

ACKNOWLEDGEMENTS & CREDITS

Recipes supplied by:

Donna Baker
Lynn Baygan
Veronica Betancourt
Rosie Bialowas
Lena Cederham Birnbaum
Pam Blanton
Joan Bogdan
Susan Burnside
Lucy Carney
Alain Cohen
Alice Colin

Lane Crowther
Heidi Daizell
Robin Davis
Tony DiSalvo
Dorothy Duder
Lucy Footlik
Karen Hallal
Dawn Hansen
Ginny Leith Holland
Sheryl Hurd-House
Wendy Hutzler
Karen Kaplan

Shari Kaplan
Jeanne Thiel Kelly
Kristine Kidd
Celester Kuch
Tammy Moore-Worthington
Selma Brown Morrow
Atsuko Osawa
Leslie Paris Patson
Diane Sandoval
Carolyn Schmitz
Rachel Shakerchi
Leslie Sheehan

Leigh Ann Shevchik
Helene Siegel
Rick Skelton
Scott Snyder
Christine Stack
Sofia Stamos
Greetha Subramanian
Sarah Tenaglia
Joanne Weir
Arthur Wenner

Concept:
Tamra Febesh
Amy G. Bigerna

Editorial development and original writing:
Norman Kolpas

Graphic design:
Sandy Douglas

Illustrations:
Michelle Burchard

Index:
Barbara Wurf

Proofreader:
Katie Goldman

Rights and permissions:
Sybil Shimazu Neubauer

Typography:
TeleText Typography, Inc.